THE ULTIMATE

BOOK OF

FAMILY
CARD
GAMES

STERLING CHILDREN'S BOOKS
New York

An Imprint of Sterling Publishing
387 Park Avenue South
New York, NY 10016

ISBN 978-1-4027-5041-0

Distributed in Canada by Sterling Publishing
c/o Canadian Manda Group, 165 Dufferin Street
Toronto, Ontario, Canada M6K 3H6
Distributed in the United Kingdom by GMC Distribution Services
Castle Place, 166 High Street, Lewes, East Sussex, England BN7 1XU
Distributed in Australia by Capricorn Link (Australia) Pty. Ltd.
P.O. Box 704, Windsor, NSW 2756, Australia

For information about custom editions, special sales, and premium
and corporate purchases, please contact Sterling Special Sales
at 800-805-5489 or specialsales@sterlingpublishing.com.

Designed by Rae Ann Spitzenberger

Printed in China
Lot #:
12 14 15 13 11
10/18
www.sterlingpublishing.com/kids

THE
ULTIMATE
BOOK OF
FAMILY
CARD
GAMES

OLIVER HO

STERLING CHILDREN'S BOOKS
New York

♥ ♣ CONTENTS ♦ ♠

INTRODUCTION

Welcome to *The Ultimate Book of Card Games for Kids*! This book presents some of the greatest card games from around the world. All you need to get started is a deck of cards (sometimes more than one).

◆◆◆

FLEXIBILITY: THE RULES ARE ALWAYS CHANGING

The best way to learn these games is to play them. Unless a game is being played at a tournament, there are rarely "official" rules. Instead, people play by the rules they learned from someone else, who learned them from someone else, and so on. That is why the rules are flexible. The rules in this book are meant to introduce the basic idea of each game.

After playing a game for a while, it's often fun to come up with new versions of the game. That's how games evolve.

If you play enough of the games, you will begin to notice similarities between some of them. For example, there are several games where players try to win "tricks." Learning strategies for one game may be useful in playing similar games. Strategies are developed by seeing what helps or hurts other players during a game.

TYPES OF GAMES: HOW THIS BOOK IS ORGANIZED

There are many different types of card games. This book will introduce some of the most common types, and for each type, there are easy, medium, and hard games to try.

Read over the rules for a game carefully, and then try playing a few test games, checking the rules during play. After a few games, the rules should be easy to remember.

Here's a brief description of the five categories of games in this book:

CAPTURING

The goal is to collect as many cards or points as possible, or to find and keep the specific cards needed to win or score points.

SHEDDING

The goal is to get rid of cards as quickly as possible.

PATIENCE

These games often require players to arrange cards in a special pattern on the table, and to move cards from section to section of the pattern, according to the specific rules of the game.

RUMMY

The goal is to create special combinations of cards (often known as "melds"). These games can be more challenging.

TRICK-TAKING

The goal is to win "tricks." A trick is a round (see the Glossary for a description of a "round") in which each player lays one card faceup on the table and the highest card wins. There are special rules in each game about what makes one card worth more than another. These games are often more challenging.

This classification of the games is unofficial, and some of the games in this book could fit in more than one category. For example, the game Go Fish involves shedding cards, but it also requires capturing cards. These categories are designed to give new players an idea of the main types of games and their strategies.

GLOSSARY

The words below refer to various aspects of card games. They might not be commonly known words. It's important for players to use the same words to describe key aspects of the game so that everyone understands what's happening and enjoys playing.

This book uses these words consistently; but, some games so often use different words to describe the same things that, in those cases, the more common usages will be mentioned in the rules for those games.

The Deck: Sides, Ranks, and Suits

A deck contains fifty-two cards and two jokers. Most games don't use the jokers, so set them aside unless the rules say otherwise. Some games don't even use an entire deck. In those cases, the rules will explain which cards to use for the game.

Each card in a deck has a front and a back. The front is known as the "face" of the card, and it shows the card's "rank" and "suit." The back of the card usually shows a design of some kind.

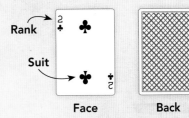

Rank

Suit

Face   Back

The rank refers to a card's ordered position within its suit. Ranks are important because some games depend on having cards with higher or lower ranks. If a card has a number on it, it is called a "number card," and that number is its rank. If a card is a jack, queen, or king, it is called a "face card" (because they usually have pictures of people on them), and the letter on its face is its rank. For example, the 2 of hearts has a rank of 2. The king (K) of clubs has a rank of K.

Aces may be "low" or "high," depending on the game. When the rules say that aces are high, it means that the ace is the highest-ranked card in the deck, and the order of cards from highest to lowest is ace-king-queen-jack-10-9-8-7-6-5-4-3-2. When the rules say that aces are low, it means that the ace is the lowest-ranked card in the deck, and the order of cards from highest to lowest is king-queen-jack-10-9-8-7-6-5-4-3-2-ace. In many games, aces can be played as either high or low, depending on how a player wants to use them. This means a player could use an ace to be lower than a 2 or higher than a king. Face cards are sometimes counted as 13-12-11 for king-queen-jack. In a particular game, the rules of play may also establish that the face cards have no rank.

There are four suits in a deck: diamonds, hearts, clubs, and spades. Every rank appears in every suit. This means there are four aces (the ace of diamonds, ace of hearts, ace of clubs, and ace of spades), four kings, four queens, and so on. In many games, it's important to pay attention to a card's suit. The rules will explain how suits are important in a particular game.

The rules will often instruct whether cards should be "faceup" or "facedown." If a card is faceup, it means everyone can see its rank and suit. If a card is facedown, it means the back of the card is visible and the rank and suit are hidden.

Shuffling

There are several different ways to shuffle, and new players usually learn how to shuffle by watching more experienced players do it. The purpose of shuffling is to mix up the order of the cards so that no one knows which cards will be dealt.

One very simple way to do this is to place the deck facedown on the table and spread the cards around in a random mess with both hands, making sure to keep all of the cards facedown. After jumbling them like this for a while, gather them all up into a neat, facedown stack.

Cutting

Another way to mix up the cards is to cut the deck. There are two steps to cutting. Start with the deck in a neat, facedown stack. For the first step, lift about half of the cards and place them to one side.

Then pick up the rest of the cards (the cards that were the bottom half of the stack), and place them on top of the cards that were placed to one side in the first step.

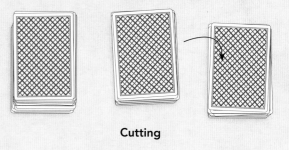

Cutting

Dealing

Most card games require one player to be the "dealer." This is the person who holds the deck and gives cards to each player. Often, the dealer is also the person in charge of the game, who makes decisions on any questions about rules that come up during the game.

There are many ways to pick a dealer. One is to have each player choose one card from the facedown deck. Then, the person who has the highest or lowest card becomes the dealer. Another way is that one player can simply volunteer to deal.

When dealing, hold the cards facedown in a neat stack in one hand. Then, with the other hand, lift the top card, keeping it facedown, and place it on the table in front of a player.

Usually, a dealer gives one card facedown to each player, going around the table in order. She deals herself the last card. She then deals the first player again and repeats the process until everyone has the number of cards they need for the game.

For most games, when a new round begins (see below for a definition of a "round"), the deal moves to the player whose turn occurred after the dealer of the previous round. This way, the deal moves around the table. If a game does not follow this pattern, the rules will specify the difference.

Hand

The group of cards a player is dealt at the start of a game is called his "hand," and a player might add or remove cards from his hand during a game. At the start of a game, unless the rules say otherwise, these cards should be kept facedown on the table until the player picks them up—then the player should make sure no one else can see what cards he has been dealt.

Round

Many games are made up of several "rounds" or cycles of play. Usually, at the start of each round, each player is dealt a hand of cards. Then there is some type of game play and an end to the round. For example, a round might end by everyone giving his or her cards back to the dealer,

who shuffles the deck and prepares to start a new round of the game.

Stock Pile

In many games, after the dealer has given players their cards, he places the rest of the deck on the table in a neat pile, and during the game, players will take cards from this pile as described in the rules. This pile of cards is sometimes created in different ways, but the main idea is that many games require a stack of cards from which players will take cards. This pile is most often called the "stock" or "stock pile."

Drawing

Many games require players to take cards from the stock, another player's hand, or another source such as a discard or pickup pile. Usually, the action of taking a card is called "drawing" a card.

Discarding/Playing/Shedding

When a player places a card from his hand on the table, it can be called "discarding," "playing," or "shedding" a card, depending on the game. If there is a discard pile, the rules specify how it is created. A discard pile is different from the stock pile (see above for a definition of "stock pile").

Taking Turns

For most games, each player takes one turn before play passes to the next player. Following the deal, the first player to take a turn is usually the person who sits on the dealer's left. The next turn usually goes to the person on the left of the previous player, and so on around the table. If a game does not follow this pattern, the rules will specify the difference.

Common Combinations

Many games make reference to certain combinations of cards.

♦ **PAIR:** Two cards with the same rank, such as two 8s.

♦ **THREE OF A KIND:** Three cards with the same rank, such as three jacks.

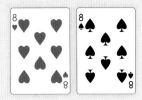

♦ **FOUR OF A KIND:** Four cards with the same rank, such as four aces.

♦ **FLUSH:** A certain number of cards (specified in the rules) that have the same suit. The ranks don't matter. An example of a flush could be the 3 of clubs, 7 of clubs, and jack of clubs.

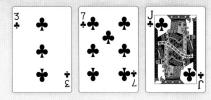

All cards in a flush have the same suit.

Layout

Some games require players to place cards on the table in a specific pattern, often called a "layout." If a game uses a different name for this, the rules will specify the difference.

Behavior

It's important to know the rules of a game and for all players to agree on the rules before starting. If any questions about the rules come up during a game, it's a good idea to check the rules in this book.

It's common for players to change rules to a game, once they've become used to it and see ways that could make it more interesting. If you want to do this, make sure all the players agree on the changes before you play.

When playing, always be polite to the other players, and don't cheat. The most common way to cheat is to try to see what cards another player is holding in his hand. Cheating makes a game less fun for everyone.

Remember also that these are games, and winning or losing isn't something to get upset about. If you see that someone is getting upset about losing, it's usually a good idea to suggest playing a different game.

CHAPTER 1

CAPTURING GAMES

BEGGAR-MY-NEIGHBOR

TYPE OF GAME: CAPTURING	**NUMBER OF PLAYERS:** 2 (with one deck of cards) or up to 6 (with two decks shuffled together)

OBJECT: Capture all the cards

Capturing games have always been popular, and this is one of the oldest of them.

HOW TO PLAY

Deal out all the cards. It's okay if some players have a few cards more or less than others. Players should keep their cards in a facedown stack on the table. Players can't look at their cards before playing.

In this game, the cards fall into two groups depending on their ranks (the suits don't matter in this game):

♦ **PAY CARDS:** Jack, queen, and king (also known as face cards), and the ace

♦ **SPOT CARDS:** Cards 2 through 10 (also known as number cards)

In turn, each player turns over the top card from his stack and places it faceup in a single pile on the table. All players place cards onto the same pile, so it should be within reach of everyone.

As long as players turn up spot cards, everyone keeps taking turns.

When a player turns up a pay card, the other players must place (or "pay out") cards from their stacks faceup onto the faceup pile. The number of cards paid out depends on the rank of the pay card that is turned up, in this manner:

♦ **JACK:** Everyone else pays out one card onto the pile.

♦ **QUEEN:** Everyone else pays out two cards.

♦ **KING:** Everyone else pays out three cards.

♦ **ACE:** Everyone else pays out four cards.

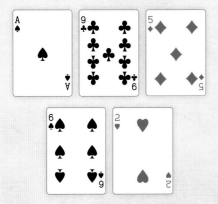

If all the cards that everyone pays out are spot cards, then the player who dealt the pay card wins the entire pile of faceup cards on the table. That player gathers up the pile, turns it facedown, and adds it to the bottom of her stack.

While paying out cards, if another pay card is played, then it cancels out the previous pay card, and all the other players must now pay out their cards according to the rank of the new pay card.

Here's an example of a payout, in a game with two players:

♦ **PLAYER 1:** Turns up a king.

♦ **PLAYER 2:** Start paying out three cards. While doing this, he turns up an ace. This cancels out the previous pay card (the king).

♦ **PLAYER 1:** Start paying out four cards. While doing this, she turns up a jack. This cancels out the previous pay card (the ace)

♦ **PLAYER 2:** Pays out one card. The card he pays out is a spot card.

♦ **PLAYER 1:** Gathers up the entire faceup pile from the table, turns it facedown, and adds it to the bottom of the stack she was dealt at the start of the game. Then she starts a new faceup pile on the table by dealing out the top card from her stack.

Play continues until one of the players "beggars" all of the others, by capturing all the cards. The player who captures all the cards wins the game.

LEVEL:
EASY | GOPS

TYPE OF GAME: CAPTURING   **NUMBER OF PLAYERS:** 2 or 3

OBJECT: Capture diamonds that add up to the most points

GOPS is an acronym that stands for "Game of Pure Strategy."

HOW TO PLAY
Separate the deck into four piles, arranged by suit: one pile of diamonds, one pile of hearts, one pile of clubs, and one pile of spades.

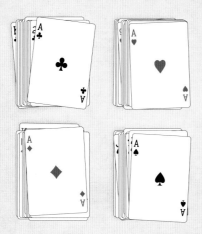

Shuffle each pile separately, and then place each pile facedown on the table. Make sure to set the pile of diamonds in the center of the table. This will be the stock.

Give one of the other suit piles to each player. This will be that player's hand. If there are only two players, set the leftover pile aside—it won't be used.

At the start of each round, turn the top card of the stock faceup. Each player then looks at his hand, chooses a card, and places it facedown on the table. This is called the "bid" card.

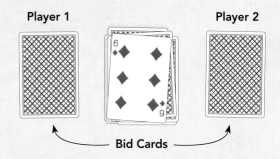

Player 1   **Player 2**

Bid Cards

After everyone has placed bid cards on the table, everyone turns them faceup at the same time. The player with the highest-ranked card wins the diamond that is faceup on the stock, and the round ends. In this game, aces are low.

The winner of this diamond places it on the table in front of her, creating a stack of diamonds as the game continues. Set the bid cards aside in a discard pile. Players then start a new round by turning over the top card in the stock.

In a two-player game, if there's a tie between the bids, set the bid cards aside in the discard pile, and leave the diamond on top of the stock. No one wins it, and players make another bid.

In a three-player game, if two players tie, then the third player wins the diamond regardless of the rank of his card. If all three players tie, set the bid cards aside in the discard pile, and leave the diamond on top of the stock. No one wins it, and players make another bid.

The game continues until players have used up all of the cards from their original piles. If there is a tie between the last bids, no one wins that diamond.

When players have used up all their cards, the game ends, and it's time to find out who has the highest-valued diamonds. Each player looks at the diamonds they've won, and totals their worth:

- ♦ **ACE:** 1 point
- ♦ **NUMBER CARDS:** Points equal the value of their ranks, for example, 2s are worth 2 points, 3s are worth 3 points, and so on.
- ♦ **JACK:** 11 points
- ♦ **QUEEN:** 12 points
- ♦ **KING:** 13 points

The player with the most points wins the game.

♦♦♦

LEVEL:
EASY

NINETY-NINE

TYPE OF GAME: CAPTURING   **NUMBER OF PLAYERS:** 3 to 13

OBJECT: Capture all the counters from the other players

This game adds a fun twist by using counters, or tokens, that players try to win.

HOW TO PLAY

Each player will need three counters. Any small objects, such as coins or candies, will do.

Deal three cards to each player, and leave the rest of the deck facedown as the stock.

When it's a player's turn, she places one of her cards faceup on the table, states the total value of all the cards played so far, and then takes a new card from the stock.

Before the first card is played, the value of the faceup pile is 0. Then as each player adds a card, the type of card that's played changes the value of the pile. Players must be able to add and subtract numbers quickly—it may help to have a pen and some paper handy to keep track of the values during a game:

♦ **ACE OF CLUBS OR ACE OF SPADES:** Changes the value of the pile to any number the player chooses, between 0 and 99.

If someone plays one of these aces, they decide how much the pile is worth.

♦ **ACE OF DIAMONDS OR ACE OF HEARTS:** Increases the value by 2.

♦ **3 OR 4 OF ANY SUIT:** No change.

♦ **ANY 5:** Increases the value by 5.

♦ **ANY 6:** Increases the value by 6.

♦ **ANY 7:** Increases the value by 7.

♦ **ANY 8:** Increases the value by 8.

♦ **ANY 9:** Changes the value to 99.

♦ **ANY 10:** Lowers the value by 10.

♦ **ANY JACK:** Increases the value by 10, and changes the direction of play.

(After playing a jack, the next player to take a turn is the one who played the card before the jack was played, and so on in that direction.)

A jack increases the value of the pile by ten and changes the direction of play.

♦ **ANY QUEEN OR KING:** Increases the value by 10.

The total value of the pile cannot go over 99. The first player who can't play a card without going over 99 loses a counter (token) to the previous player, and the round ends.

Start a new round by gathering up all the cards and dealing new hands to everyone. The player who captures all the counters from the other players wins the game.

SLAPJACK

TYPE OF GAME: CAPTURING   **NUMBER OF PLAYERS:** 2 to 10

OBJECT: Capture all the cards

This is a fast and physical game in which the player with the quickest hands (and mind) usually wins.

HOW TO PLAY

Deal out all the cards. It's okay if some players have a few cards more or less than others. Players should keep their cards in a facedown stack on the table or in their hand. Players can't look at their cards before playing.

In turn, each player turns over the top card from his stack and places it faceup in a single pile on the table. All players place cards onto the same pile, so it should be within reach of everyone.

It's important that no players, not even the one who's taking the turn, see the card before it lands faceup on the table. The best way to do this is to lift the card from your stack, keeping the card facedown, and move it over to the pile on the table. Then flip it over quickly and drop it faceup onto the pile.

Each player follows in turn, lifting the top card from his hand and dropping it faceup onto the pile.

When a jack turns up, that's when the race begins. The first player to slap his palm on it wins the entire pile of faceup cards. That player gathers up the pile, turns it facedown, and adds it to the bottom of his stack.

If any players run out of cards, they can still play by watching for a jack to be played onto the faceup pile and then trying to slap the pile first when it happens.

Watch out! When a jack is played, the quickest player to slap the pile wins.

If a player slaps a card that isn't a jack, that player must give his top card facedown to the next player, who adds it to the bottom of her stack. By pretending to slap the pile, players can try to trick each other into slapping the faceup pile when no jack has been played.

The player who captures all the cards wins the game.

SNAP

TYPE OF GAME: CAPTURING   **NUMBER OF PLAYERS:** 2 to 8

OBJECT: Capture all the cards

This fast-paced game is similar to Slapjack. But a couple of changes make playing Snap even more frantic.

HOW TO PLAY

Deal out all the cards. It's okay if some players have a few cards more or less than others. Players should keep their cards in a facedown stack or, for a faster-paced game, hold the stack in their hand. Players can't look at their cards before playing.

In turn, each player turns over the top card from his stack and places it faceup in a single pile on the table. All players place cards onto the same pile, so it should be within reach of everyone.

As in Slapjack, it's important that no players, not even the one who's taking the turn, see the card before it lands faceup on the table. The best way to do this is to lift the card from your stack, keeping the card facedown, and move it over to the pile on the table. Then flip it over quickly and drop it faceup onto the pile.

Each player follows in turn, lifting the top card from his hand and dropping it faceup onto the pile. Everyone needs to watch out for a card to be played that matches the rank of the previous card. For example, if the top card on the faceup pile is a king, and the next player drops another

king onto the pile, then whoever calls out "Snap!" first wins the entire pile of faceup cards. That player gathers up the pile, turns it facedown, and adds it to the bottom of his stack.

Unlike Slapjack, any players who run out of cards during Snap are out for the rest of the game.

When a new card is placed on the faceup pile that is the same rank as the card on top of the pile, the players should race to say "Snap!" first.

If a player calls out "Snap!" by mistake (if the newest faceup card doesn't match the rank of the previous faceup card), or if more than one player calls out "Snap!" at exactly the same time, then the entire faceup pile is placed to one side, still faceup. This pile is called the "pool." Then with the next player's turn, a new faceup pile starts, and the game continues as usual.

When a card turns up on the new faceup pile that matches the rank of the top card of the pool, the first player to call out "Snap pool!" wins the pool. If a player calls "Snap pool!" by mistake, or if more than one player calls it at exactly the same time, then the new faceup pile is added to the top of the pool, and yet another faceup pile is started with the next player's turn.

The player who captures all the cards wins the game.

◆ ◆ ◆

EASY | WAR

♣

TYPE OF GAME: CAPTURING   **NUMBER OF PLAYERS:** 2

OBJECT: Capture all the cards

Sometimes this simple game is called Everlasting because it can go on for a long time.

HOW TO PLAY

Split the deck evenly, so each player has twenty-six cards. Players must hold their cards in a facedown stack and can't look at their cards.

Both players turn over their top cards at the same time, and place them on the table in front of them. Aces are high, and suits don't matter. The player with the highest-ranked card takes both cards from the table and adds them facedown to the bottom of his stack of cards. This is one round.

If players turn over cards with the same rank, such as two 10s, then it's a tie, and those two cards are left faceup. Each player then places the next three cards from her stack facedown on the table next to the tied cards. The game continues as before, and whoever wins the next round also wins the tied cards, plus the facedown cards next to them.

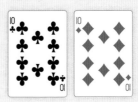

When two cards of the same rank are played by both players, the "war" begins.

If there's a tie, and it's followed by another tie, the cards in the second tie are also set aside, together with three more facedown cards from each player and so on until one player finally wins a round. (That player also wins all the tied cards and the facedown cards.)

The player who captures all the cards wins the game.

EGYPTIAN RATSCREW

TYPE OF GAME: CAPTURING   **NUMBER OF PLAYERS:** 2 or more

OBJECT: Capture all the cards

This game combines elements of Slapjack and Beggar-My-Neighbor.

HOW TO PLAY

Deal out all the cards. It's okay if some players have a few cards more or less than others. Players should keep their cards in a facedown stack on the table. Players can't look at their cards before playing.

In turn, each player turns over the top card from his stack and places it faceup in a single pile on the table. All players place cards onto the same pile, so it should be within reach of everyone.

As in Slapjack, it's important that no players, not even the one who's taking the turn, see the card before it lands faceup on the table. The best way to do this is to lift the card from your stack, keeping the card facedown, and move it over to the pile on the table. Then flip it over quickly and drop it faceup onto the pile.

Each player follows in turn, lifting the top card from his hand and dropping it faceup onto the pile. Players need to pay attention to every card that is played. In the simplest version of this game, when two cards with the same rank (such as two 8s, or two queens) are played one right

after the other, then the first player to slap her palm on top of the faceup pile captures the entire pile. That player gathers up the pile, turns it facedown, and adds it to the bottom of her stack.

If any player slaps the faceup pile at the wrong time (when the combination of cards doesn't allow it), that player must take two cards from his stack and place them facedown on the table next to the faceup pile. These are the "penalty" cards. Whoever wins the faceup pile next also wins the penalty cards.

In this game, players can win both the faceup pile and the facedown "penalty" pile.

If any players run out of cards, they can still play by watching for the right combination of cards to be played onto the faceup pile and then trying to slap the pile first when it happens.

The player who captures all the cards wins the game.

KEMPS

TYPE OF GAME: CAPTURING	**NUMBER OF PLAYERS:** 2, 3, or 4 teams of 2 players each (4, 6, or 8 players)

OBJECT: Capture all four cards of a same rank (known as "four of a kind"); figure out when your opponents do or don't have four of a kind; and avoid losing enough rounds as a team to spell out the word K-E-M-P-S (one letter for each game lost).

This game involves quick-thinking, sneaky team play, and a loud voice.

HOW TO PLAY

Begin by picking teams. Each team should then meet in private to come up with secret signals.

Teammates need these signals to let each other know when one of them has four cards of a same rank, for example, four aces. When a teammate sees the signal, he yells "Kemps!" If someone on another team spots the signal first, she can yell "Stop Kemps!"

The signal must be visual, such as a wink, a facial expression, or a gesture. The signal can't be verbal—in other words, players can't use words or sounds as signals.

Pick one player to be the dealer. After each round, the player sitting to the dealer's left becomes the new dealer.

Deal four cards to each player. Then deal four more cards in a row faceup on the table. As soon as the last card has been dealt in this faceup row, any player may pick up any number of the faceup cards from the table and add them to his hand. In this game, players don't take turns. As soon as a player sees a card she wants, she should take it. If two players want

the same faceup card, the card goes to the first player to touch it. A player can try to confuse another player by reaching for one card, and then at the last moment taking a different one.

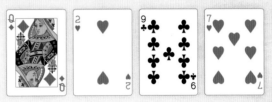

As soon as a player sees a card he wants in the faceup row, he should take it.

Whenever a player picks up a card from the table, he must replace it with a card from his hand. Players should always have exactly four cards in their hands, and there should always be a row of four cards faceup on the table.

Players continue picking up and discarding cards as many times as they want until no one wants any of the four faceup cards. The dealer then removes the four faceup cards and sets them aside in a facedown pile. These cards won't be used again until the round ends, when they'll be gathered up and shuffled back into the deck.

The dealer now deals out four new cards from the deck faceup on the table, and play resumes, with players picking up cards and replacing them with cards from their hands.

The game continues this way until someone yells "Kemps!" or "Stop Kemps!" This signals the end of the round.

A round also ends when no one wants any of the faceup cards, there aren't any more cards in the deck to deal out, and no one calls "Kemps!" or "Stop Kemps!" In these situations, the round ends with no winner. A new player becomes the dealer, and that person gathers up all the cards, shuffles the deck, and starts a new round by dealing out four new cards to each player and four more cards in a row faceup on the table.

Yelling Kemps

If a player thinks her partner has four of a kind, she yells "Kemps!" If anyone thinks someone on the other team(s) has four of a kind, that person yells "Stop Kemps!"

Then one of these things happens:

♦ The partner of the person who called "Kemps!" must show his cards. If he has four of a kind, the other team(s) receives one of the letters in the word "Kemps," starting with "K." If he does not have four of a kind, then the team that incorrectly called "Kemps!" receives a letter.

♦ If someone calls "Stop Kemps!" and either player on the team that is called actually has four of a kind, then that team receives a letter. If someone calls "Stop Kemps!" and no one on the team that is called has four of a kind, then the team that called "Stop Kemps!" receives a letter.

After someone yells "Kemps!" or "Stop Kemps!" and the letter is given to a team, the round ends. A new player becomes the dealer, and that person gathers up all the cards, shuffles the deck, and starts a new round by dealing out four new cards to each player.

Between hands, teams may leave for a few moments to come up with new signals. This is usually a good idea if a team thinks that their opponents have figured out their signals.

The first team to lose enough rounds to spell the word K-E-M-P-S loses the game.

STRATEGIES

♦ The best signals are simple, small, and natural, such as a yawn or a blink.

♦ Players should be subtle about which cards they are collecting.

♦ Players should watch the other team to try to learn their signals.

♦ Players may try to confuse another team by picking up cards they don't need. Players should pay attention to see if cards that were picked up are discarded later.

♦ If a player figures out what cards his partner wants (by observing which cards his partner picks up), he should discard those cards to help his partner. For example, if a player holds an ace in his hand, and notices that his partner is picking up aces, he should try discarding the ace to see if that helps his partner.

♦ Players may use fake signals to trick another team into yelling "Stop Kemps!"

KNACK

TYPE OF GAME: CAPTURING   **NUMBER OF PLAYERS:** 2 to 8

OBJECT: Trade for cards to create a hand that has a value of 31 points or as close to 31 as possible (and in one special case, 32 points); win all of the other players' counters; and be the last player left in the game.

This game uses some elements from Ninety-Nine. It's popular in Germany, where it's also known as Schwimmen, the German word for "swimming."

HOW TO PLAY

Each player will need three counters. Any small objects, such as coins or candies, will do.

Go through the deck and set aside all number cards lower than 7. This should leave a deck of thirty-two cards. Aces are high.

Pick one player to be the dealer. After each round, the player sitting to the dealer's left becomes the new dealer. If there are only two players, they take turns dealing each round.

Deal three cards to each player. Then deal three more cards in a row facedown on the table. The cards in this row are called the "spare" hand.

Now the dealer has the choice of exchanging her own three cards for the spare hand. The dealer can only do this once, right after dealing to everyone. Also, the dealer can look at her cards first, but cannot look at the cards in the spare hand.

After the dealer makes this decision (to exchange all her cards for the spare hand, or not), she then turns the three cards in the spare hand faceup, so everyone can see them.

Taking turns, each player chooses whether he wants to take one spare card and leave one from his hand in its place, or if he wants to pass. Players can't pick up and then replace the same card during their turn. The spare hand will always contain three cards.

If all the players pass, the dealer picks up the spare hand, and sets those cards aside facedown in a pile. Then she deals three new cards faceup on the table, making a new spare hand.

This continues until all the cards in the deck have been used up, or until someone believes he has the best hand. The object is to create a hand that has a value of 31 points or as close to 31 as possible (and in one special case, 32 points). A player signals this by knocking on the table.

If the player who knocks has a hand totaling exactly 31 or 32 points, he reveals his hand, and all the other players give one of their counters to him.

If a player decides she has enough points, but does not have a hand totaling exactly 31 or 32 points, then she knocks but keeps her cards hidden. Then everyone else takes one more turn, choosing to exchange one card with one in the spare hand or to pass. Then all the players show their cards. The player with the hand that comes closest to 31 points wins the round, and the player with the lowest-scoring hand must give a counter to the winning player.

Values of Hands

♦ **THREE OF A KIND (NOT THREE ACES):** 30½ points

♦ **THREE ACES (AUTOMATICALLY WINS THE ROUND, ALL PLAYERS MUST GIVE A COUNTER TO THAT PLAYER):** 32 points

A hand of three aces equals 32 points and automatically wins the round.

♦ **FLUSH (THREE CARDS OF THE SAME SUIT):** The value is equal to the three cards added together.

Values of Cards

♦ **ACE:** 11 points

♦ **KING, QUEEN, OR JACK:** 10 points

♦ **NUMBER CARDS:** Points equal the value of their ranks. For example, 2s are worth 2 points, 3s are worth 3 points, and so on.

If a player doesn't have three of a kind or a flush, then the value of her hand is the value of the highest single card she's holding. For example, if she's holding the 9 of diamonds, 7 of hearts, and 10 of spades, then the value of her hand is 10 points.

Suits only have value in the case of a tie. Then, the hand with the most cards in the highest-value suit wins. Clubs are the highest, followed by spades, then hearts, and then diamonds.

When a player loses all three of his counters, he's "swimming" and can continue playing until he loses one more time. Then he's out of the game.

The winner is the player who wins all the other players' counters.

BASRA

TYPE OF GAME: CAPTURING   **NUMBER OF PLAYERS:** 2

OBJECT: Capture cards to earn 101 points before anyone else

This game is popular throughout the Middle East, especially in Egypt and Lebanon.

HOW TO PLAY

Deal four cards to each player. Then deal four more cards in a row faceup on the table. This row is called the "floor."

If any of the cards on the floor is a jack of any suit, or the 7 of diamonds, the dealer takes these cards, mixes them back into the deck, and deals new cards from the top of the pack to replace them.

Players take turns trying to capture cards that are "on the floor." If a player plays a card that doesn't capture anything, it stays on the floor next to the others and becomes available for capture itself. This is called "trailing" a card.

A player plays one card from his hand faceup on the table, and if he is able, uses one of three capturing methods: matching cards, adding up cards, or both.

♦ **MATCHING:** If the player's card has the same rank as one of the cards on the floor, he captures it.

For example, if the 2 of hearts is among the cards on the floor, and a player plays the 2 of clubs, he captures the 2 of hearts. A player's card can only capture one card at a time from the floor with this method. In the above example, if the 2 of diamonds and 2 of hearts were on the floor, and the player played the 2 of clubs, he could only capture one of the 2s from the floor, not both.

♦ **ADDING:** If the ranks of any number of cards on the floor can be added up to equal the rank of the player's card, then all of those cards are captured.

For example, if the 7 of clubs and 3 of hearts are among the cards on the floor, and a player plays the 10 of spades, she captures the 7 of clubs and the 3 of hearts (because 7 + 3 = 10). In this example, the 7 of clubs and 3 of hearts are called a "set."

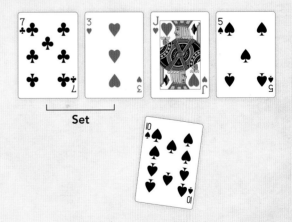

7 + 3 = 10. This means that if a player has a 10 of spades, he can capture both the 7 and 3.

Points are counted in this way:

♦ **ACE:** 1 point

♦ **NUMBER CARDS:** The value of their ranks, for example, 2s are worth 2 points, 3s are worth 3 points, and so on.

♦ **KING OR QUEEN:** 0 points. It's important to note that queens and kings don't have a rank in this game.

A queen can only be captured by another queen, and a king by another king, unless a jack or the 7 of diamonds is played (see the rules for this below).

If there is more than one set of cards on the table that add up to the value of the card played, all of the sets are captured. For example, suppose that among the cards on the floor there are the 2 of hearts, 2 of diamonds, 2 of clubs, 5 of spades, and ace of diamonds. If a player plays the 6 of diamonds, she captures all five cards on the floor, because 2 + 2 + 2 = 6, and 5 + 1 (the ace) = 6.

When capturing sets of cards by adding, each captured card can only be part of one set. For example, suppose that among the cards on the floor there are the 2 of hearts, 2 of diamonds, 2 of clubs, and 4 of diamonds. If a player plays the 6 of diamonds, he must choose either to capture the set of three 2s (because 2 + 2 + 2 = 6) or the set containing one 2 and the 4 of diamonds (because 4 + 2 = 6).

♦ **MATCHING AND ADDING:** Players may make more than one type of capture in the same turn.

For example, if the 7 of clubs, 3 of hearts, and 10 of diamonds are among the cards on the floor, and a player plays the 10 of clubs, he captures the 7 of clubs, 3 of

hearts, and 10 of diamonds (because 7 + 3 = 10, and the 10 of diamonds matches his 10 of clubs).

Every player must play a card when it's his turn. If a player's card captures any of the cards on the floor, she gathers those cards, along with the card she played from her hand, and places them facedown in a pile in front of her. This is called her "capture" pile.

Players do not have to capture cards on their turns, even if they are holding cards that can make captures. For example, a player may want to save higher-ranked cards for later in the game, so he can capture more cards from the floor with the adding method.

However, if a card is played (that is, placed on the table) that can make a capture, the player must collect the cards and place them in his capture pile.

If a player captures all of the cards on the floor, except as described below, this is called a "basra," and the player earns an extra 10 points at the end of the round.

When a basra is scored, the player should place the card that did the capturing faceup in her capture pile, so she will remember it at the end of the round.

Playing Jacks and the 7 of Diamonds

A jack of any suit captures all of the cards on the floor, but this kind of capture doesn't count as a basra, and the player doesn't earn extra points.

The 7 of diamonds also wins every card on the floor. In one case this counts as a basra, but in another it doesn't, according to these rules:

♦ If the cards on the floor all have a rank (this means, for this game, that there are no queens or kings on the floor), and they add up to 10 or less, then it counts as a basra.

♦ If the floor cards add up to more than 10, or if there are any queens or kings on the floor, the 7 of diamonds still captures all the cards, but it doesn't count as a basra.

If a jack or the 7 of diamonds is played when the floor is empty (because all the floor cards have already been captured), the card stays there and can be captured in a future turn.

After all the players use up the four cards they were originally dealt, the dealer gives four new cards to each player, and the game continues.

When the entire deck has been used up, and no one has any cards left in their hands, then the round is over.

Any cards left on the floor at this point go to the player who last made a capture, but this doesn't count as a basra.

Now players count up their captured cards:

♦ The player with the most cards wins 30 points. If it's a tie, the 30 points are held for the next round. The player who wins that round will then win 60 points. If that next round ends in another tie, those 60 points are held over until the next round, when the winner will receive 90 points.

♦ Players add 1 extra point to their scores for every jack and every ace they captured, an extra 2 points for the 2 of clubs, and an extra 3 points for the 10 of diamonds. And 10 points are added for every basra.

Whoever reaches 101 points first wins the game. If both players reach 101 in the same round, they play another round (or rounds) until the tie is broken. If no one reaches 101 at the end of a round, the deal moves to the next player in turn, and a new round begins.

LEVEL: HARD	CASSINO

TYPE OF GAME: CAPTURING	**NUMBER OF PLAYERS:**	2 or 4 (2 teams of 2 players each, with teammates sitting opposite one another)

OBJECT: Capture cards and collect points

This is an Italian game from the 1700s that is related to Scopa.

HOW TO PLAY

Deal four cards to each player. Then deal four cards faceup onto the table. These four cards are called the "floor."

Players now take turns trying to capture cards that are "on the floor." A player plays one card from his hand faceup on the table, and, if he is able, uses one of four capturing methods: matching cards, adding up cards, matching and adding, or building.

♦ **MATCHING:** If the player's card has the same rank as any of the cards on the floor, he captures all the cards that match. For example, if the 2 of hearts is among the cards on the floor, and a player plays the 2 of clubs, he captures the 2 of hearts. If the 2 of hearts and the 2 of diamonds are on the floor, and the player plays the 2 of clubs, he captures both of the 2s from the floor.

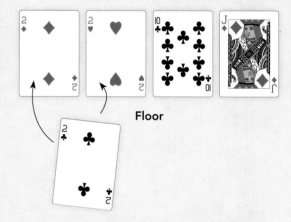

Floor

♦ **ADDING:** If the ranks of any number of cards on the floor can be added up to equal the rank of the player's card, then all of those cards are captured.

For example, if the 7 of clubs and 3 of hearts are among the cards on the floor, and a player plays the 10 of spades, she captures the 7 of clubs and the 3 of hearts (because 7 + 3 = 10). In this example, the 7 of clubs and 3 of hearts are called a "set."

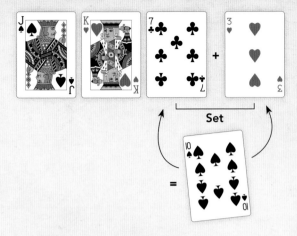

Points are counted in this manner:

- **ACE:** 1 point

- **NUMBER CARDS:** Points equal the value of their ranks. For example, 2s are worth 2 points, 3s are worth 3 points, and so on.

- **KING, QUEEN, OR JACK:** 0 points. In this game, jacks, queens, and kings don't have ranks.

For this game, a jack can only be captured by another jack, a queen by another queen, and a king by another king.

If there is more than one set of cards on the table that add up to the value of the card played, all of the sets are captured. For example, suppose that among the cards on the floor there are the 2 of hearts, 2 of diamonds, 2 of clubs, 5 of spades, and ace of diamonds. If a player plays the 6 of diamonds, she captures all five cards on the floor, because 2 + 2 + 2 = 6, and 5 + 1 (the ace) = 6.

When capturing sets of cards by adding, each captured card can only be part of one set. For example, suppose among the cards on the floor there are the 2 of hearts, 2 of diamonds, 2 of clubs, and 4 of diamonds. If a player plays the 6 of diamonds, he must

choose either to capture the set of three 2s (because 2 + 2 + 2 = 6) or the set containing one 2 and the 4 of diamonds (because 4 + 2 = 6).

- **MATCHING AND ADDING:** Players may make more than one type of capture in the same turn.

For example, if the 7 of clubs, 3 of hearts, and 10 of diamonds are among the cards on the floor, and a player plays the 10 of clubs, he captures the 7 of clubs, 3 of hearts, and 10 of diamonds (because 7 + 3 = 10, and the 10 of diamonds matches his 10 of clubs).

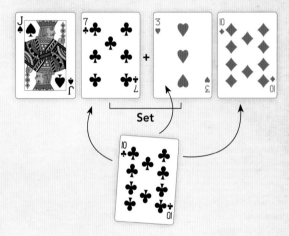

- **BUILDING:** When a player "builds" in this game, it means she is setting up cards on the table for capture by any of the three previous methods. The difference with building is that the capture happens after the player sets up cards over more than one turn.

When a player starts a build, he stacks all of the cards in the build together, leaving them faceup on the table, and states clearly what the value of the build will be. A build cannot be made entirely out of cards that are already on the table; one card must come from the player's hand. A player can only start a build if he has one card in his hand worth the value of the build, and that card is known as the "capturing card" (however, this rule has an exception during team play—see below for details).

For example, the floor shows the ace of hearts, 2 of spades, and 3 of clubs. Those cards add up to 6 (1 + 2 + 3 = 6). In her hand, a player holds the 4 of clubs and 10 of diamonds. During her turn, she plays her 4 of clubs and says, "Building ten." By playing this card, the faceup cards on the table now add up to 10 (1 + 2 + 3 + 4 = 10). In her next turn, she plays her 10 of diamonds, which adds up to the total of the ranks of the cards in her build, and captures all of those cards. In this example, she captured cards by adding. If she did not hold the capturing card (in this example it's the 10 of diamonds) at the start of her build, she would not be allowed to start making the build.

Here's another example of building to a capture: in his hand a player holds the 10 of hearts and the 10 of spades, while among the cards on the floor are the 10 of diamonds and the 10 of clubs. During his turn, he plays the 10 of hearts, placing it on top of the 10 of diamonds and the 10 of clubs in a single pile, and saying, "Building ten." In his next turn, he plays the 10 of spades on top the pile and captures all four 10s. In this example, he captured cards by matching.

Once a player announces a build, the cards in it are considered "locked in a build," and they cannot be separated. In the example above, when the player said, "Building ten," only a 10 could capture the cards in his build. However, the risk in

making a build is that any other player can capture the build with the right card.

For example, among the cards on the floor are the 3 of clubs and 6 of spades, which add up to 9 (3 + 6 = 9). A player holds the ace of diamonds and 10 of hearts. During her turn, she plays the ace of diamonds to the table and says "Building ten." The cards in her build currently equal 10 (1 + 3 + 6 = 10), and she plans to play the 10 of hearts in her next turn so she can capture all of the cards in her build. Unfortunately for her, another player has the 10 of spades in his hand. During his turn, he plays the 10 of spades onto the build and captures all of those cards.

The benefit to building is that a player may be able to capture more cards than she otherwise would in one turn. If playing with teams, partners may choose to add to each other's builds, which can increase the number of cards they capture (see the section on "adding to a build" below).

Once a build has started, players have two more options: adding to a build, or increasing a build.

♦ **ADDING TO A BUILD:** A player can add to a build that's already on the table by using a card from his hand in combination with another card that's already on the table.

For example, among the cards on the floor are the 4 of clubs, 4 of hearts, and 5 of spades. In her hand, a player holds the ace of diamonds, 6 of spades, and 10 of clubs. During her turn, she starts a build of 10 by combining the ace of diamonds with the 4 of clubs and 5 of spades. In her next turn, she combines her 6 of spades with the 4 of hearts, placing them both on top of her existing build, and announces her intention to add to it.

Remember that in individual play, she can only do this if she holds the capturing card (in this example, it's the 10 of clubs) at the start of her build. However, when players are in teams, a player can add to his partner's build without needing to have the capturing card in his hand.

For example, one player starts a build of nine. In addition to the cards in her build, there's also a 3 of spades among the cards on the floor. Her partner holds the 6 of clubs in his hand. During his turn, he plays the 6 of clubs on top of the 3 of spades, and places both cards on top of his partner's build of nine. He doesn't need to hold a 9 (a capturing card for this build) in his hand to do this because his partner has a 9 in her hand (she must have it, or else she could not have started the build).

♦ **INCREASING A BUILD:** During her turn, a player can add a card from her hand to a build that's already on the table, as long as she will be able to capture the build with her next turn.

For example, one player plays the ace of diamonds from his hand onto the 4 of spades, which is one of the cards on the floor, and says, "Building five." The next player holds the 8 of clubs and 3 of hearts. During her turn, she plays her 3 of hearts onto the previous player's build of five, and says, "Building eight." She can do this because she holds the capturing card in her hand (the 8 of clubs), and she plans to play this card during her next turn in order capture all of the cards in the build. Of course, if another player before her has an 8, he can capture the build too.

Once a build has been increased, another player can increase it again. For example, a player starts a build of five,

using the ace of spades and 4 of hearts. The next player increases it to a build of eight by adding the 3 of diamonds. The player after that could add the 2 of clubs and increase the build to ten (assuming that this player holds a 10 in his hand).

A build can only be increased if it uses the adding method to capture cards.

If a build uses matching, it cannot be increased. For example, if there's a build of three on the table, using two 3s, it is a build that uses matching, and it cannot be increased to a build of five by adding a 2 to the build.

If a build uses both (adding and matching), it cannot be increased. For example, if there's a build of eight on the table that began with by adding a 5 and 3, to which a matching 8 was added, it is still a build of eight that uses adding and matching, so it cannot be increased to a build of ten, for example, by adding a 2 to the build.

If a build uses multiple combinations of cards (in other words, if it has had cards added to it), it also cannot be increased. For example, if a player starts a build of nine by using a 4 from his hand, in combination with an ace and a 4 from the table, and then in his next turn he combines another set of cards (such as a 2 and a 7) to add to his build, then this build cannot be increased because it uses multiple combinations of cards.

A build can only be increased by a player using cards from his hand. He cannot take a card that's already on the table (either from a build or the floor) and use it to increase a build.

When a player captures a build, she can also capture any other cards on the table that match the value of her build. For example, if she's capturing a build of four, and there's a 4 on the floor, she can also take that card.

This also works for combinations of cards that are on the table. For example, if she's capturing a build of four, and there's an ace and 3 on the floor, she can also capture those cards. This does not work if the other cards on the table are already locked into builds.

If a player manages to capture all the floor cards with one turn, this is called a "sweep," and the player who does it must keep track of it (this counts 1 extra point later in the game).

If a player starts a build that is still on the table on his next turn, he has four options: he must capture the build he started, capture another build, start a new build, or increase or add to a build. He may not play a card on the table that doesn't capture or add to a build.

Every player must play a card when it's her turn. If a player's card captures any of the cards on the floor, she gathers those cards along with the card she played from her hand, and places them facedown in a pile in front of her. This is called her "capture" pile.

Players do not have to capture cards on their turns, even if they are holding cards that can make captures. For example, a player may want to save higher-ranked cards for later in the game, so he can capture more cards from the floor with the adding method.

If a player plays a card that doesn't capture anything, it stays on the floor next to the others and becomes available for capture itself. This is called "trailing" a card.

However, if a card is played (that is, placed on the table) that can make a capture, the player must collect the cards and place them in his capture pile.

After all the players use up the four cards they were originally dealt, the dealer gives four new cards to each player, and the game continues.

When the entire deck has been used up, and no one has any cards left in their hands, then the round is over.

Any cards left on the floor at this point go to the player who last made a capture, but this doesn't count as a sweep.

Now players count up their captured cards:

- ♦ **MOST CARDS OVERALL:** 3 points (if there's a tie, no one wins these points)

- ♦ **MOST SPADES OVERALL:** 1 point (if there's a tie, no one wins these points)

- ♦ **ACE:** 1 point

- ♦ **10 OF DIAMONDS**: 2 points. This card is known as "Big Cassino."

- ♦ **2 OF SPADES:** 1 point. This card is called "Little Cassino."

- ♦ **EVERY SWEEP:** 1 point

Once scores are recorded, another round begins. Keep adding to the scores at the end of each round. The first player (or team) to collect 21 points or more wins the entire game.

If there's a tie, play another round to determine the winner. If more than one player (or team) gets more than 21 points, then whoever has the highest number of points wins the game.

PISHTI

TYPE OF GAME: CAPTURING	**NUMBER OF PLAYERS:**	4 (individually or in teams of two). If playing in teams, partners must sit opposite one another at the table.

OBJECT: Collect more than 101 points

The name of this popular Turkish card game means "cooked" and refers to the capture of a pile that contains only one card. It's similar to Basra and Cassino.

HOW TO PLAY

The dealer cuts the cards by lifting up about half the deck, and the player to his right takes the bottom card from the top half and places this card faceup on the table. This card is the "marker." If it's a jack, the player wins the card and places it faceup on the table as part of her "capture" pile of cards. Whenever players capture cards, they keep them faceup in this pile. Each player will have her own capture pile. If the marker was a jack, a new card is taken from the bottom of the deck to become the marker card.

The dealer gathers up the rest of the deck and deals four cards facedown to each player. Then he deals four cards faceup in a stack on the table. These cards are the "pool." Finally, the dealer places the rest of the deck facedown on top of the marker. He should make sure to leave the marker sticking halfway out so everyone can see it. This card stays visible to all the players and

when the stock is later used up, the dealer will get the marker card.

The facedown pile rests on top of that marker as shown.

If the top card of the pool is a jack, the dealer wins it, and it becomes part of his capture pile. If all four faceup cards in the pool turn out to be jacks (this is very rare), the dealer gathers up everyone's cards, shuffles, and starts over.

If the top card of the pool is not a jack, then players begin taking turns trying to capture the pool. A player plays one card from his hand faceup on the table, and, if he is able, uses one of two capturing methods: matching cards or playing a jack.

♦ **MATCHING:** If the rank of the card she plays matches the rank of the card on top of the pool, she captures the pool. Otherwise, her card remains on top of the pool, and the next player takes his turn.

For example, if the top card of the pool

is the 6 of clubs, and she plays the 6 of hearts on top of it, she captures the pool.

♦ **PLAYING A JACK:** During his turn, if a player plays any jack onto the pool, he captures the pool.

When a player captures the pool, it becomes part of his capture pile. The next player then starts a new pool by playing one card faceup on the table.

Then, if the very next player then manages to win the card by matching it (that is, if she wins it without playing a jack), she wins an extra 10 points, and she must call out, "Pishti!" She places the winning card faceup next to her capture pile to mark this bonus. If she doesn't say "pishti," other players can penalize her by not allowing her the bonus points.

If the pool contains just one jack and it is captured with another jack, that's called a "Double-Pishti," and it counts for 20 extra points. The player marks this by placing both jacks faceup next to his capture pile. If the player doesn't say, "double-pishti," other players can penalize him by not allowing him to collect the bonus points.

After all the players use up the four cards they were originally dealt, the dealer gives four new cards to each player, and the game continues.

Continue playing until the deck is all used up. When the last card in the deck is reached (the marker from the start of the game), the dealer takes it.

When the entire deck has been used up, and no one has any cards left in their hands, the round ends. Any cards left in the pool at this point go to the player who last made a capture.

Now players calculate their points. Players earn points for the cards that they capture (the types of cards and the total number of cards), along with bonus points for a pishti or double-pishti:

♦ **EACH JACK:** 1 point

♦ **EACH ACE:** 1 point

♦ **2 OF CLUBS:** 2 points

♦ **10 OF DIAMONDS:** 3 points

♦ **EACH PISHTI:** 10 points

♦ **EACH DOUBLE-PISHTI:** 20 points

♦ **THE MOST CARDS:** 3 points (if there's a tie for the most cards captured, no one collects these points). Teammates combine their captured cards.

After writing down the score for each player (or combining scores for each player on a team), start a new round. Continue playing until one player (or team) collects 101 points.

OBJECT: Collect cards worth 31 points, and capture everyone else's counters

Other names for this game include Blitz, Three-Penny-Scat, and (especially in the United Kingdom) Ride the Bus.

HOW TO PLAY

Each player will need three counters. Any small objects, such as coins or candies, will do.

Deal three cards to each player. Then turn the top card of the deck faceup, and place it on the table to start an "upcard" pile. Place the rest of the deck facedown next to it—this will be the stock.

Each player begins with a hand of three cards and 3 counters.

Each player should look at the cards in her hand and start calculating how many points her cards are worth:

- ♦ **ACE:** 11 point
- ♦ **KING, QUEEN, OR JACK:** 10 points
- ♦ **NUMBER CARDS:** Points equal the value of their ranks. Tor example, 2s are worth 2 points, 3s are worth 3 points, and so on.

Suits also affect how much a hand is worth:

- ♦ **ALL THREE CARDS OF THE SAME SUIT (ALL SPADES, ALL DIAMONDS, AND SO ON):** Add up the point value for all three cards.
- ♦ **ONLY TWO CARDS ARE THE SAME SUIT:** Add up points for those cards, or use the point value of the third card if it's higher than the combined point values of the other two cards.
- ♦ **ALL THREE CARDS ARE DIFFERENT SUITS:** Use the point value of the highest single card.

The highest point value of any hand is 31. This happens if a player holds an ace, two cards worth 10 points each, and all three cards are of the same suit.

If a player's hand is worth exactly 31 points, he shows his hand immediately, wins the round, and all other players must give him a counter.

When a player "declares 31" in this way, each player must give her a counter.

If this happens to more than one player right after the cards are dealt out, all the players with 31 points win, and the others give a counter to each winner.

If no one declares 31, players begin taking turns. The goal is to build a hand that adds up to 31 points, without going over. A player follows two basic steps on her turn:

♦ **TAKE A CARD:** The player takes a card from the top of the stock pile, or from the top of the upcard pile (it's the player's choice).

♦ **SHED A CARD:** Then the player "sheds" a card by placing it on top of the upcard pile. If the player just picked up a card from the discard pile, she cannot shed the same card.

If a player's hand is worth 31 points after he picks up and sheds, he shows his hand right away, and he declares 31. He wins the round, and all the other players must give him a counter.

Players don't have to wait until they get 31 points in their hand before trying to win a round. If a player believes she has the best hand, but it is worth less than 31 points, she can choose to "knock."

To knock, the player skips her turn (she doesn't pick up or shed any cards), and she announces that she is knocking. All the other players take one more turn (each player picks up and sheds a card), and then the rounds ends. Everyone shows their cards. This is also known as a "showdown."

Each player now calculates the point value of his cards, and counters are awarded based on hands worth the lowest and highest amount of points:

♦ **LOWEST:** The player who has the hand worth the lowest amount of points loses one counter to the player who knocked.

♦ **TIE FOR LOWEST:** If there's a tie for the lowest score, the players in the tie each lose a counter to the player who knocked.

♦ **HIGHEST:** If the player who knocked has the lowest score, she gives two counters to the player with the highest score.

When a player loses all of his counters, he has one more round to continue playing. If a player ends up owing a counter again, he is out of the game. The player who captures all of the counters wins the game.

SCOPA/SCOPONE

TYPE OF GAME: CAPTURING   **NUMBER OF PLAYERS:** 2 to 4

OBJECT: Capture cards and collect 11 points

Scopa, also known as Scoop, is one of the most popular games in Italy. Scopa means "broom," the source of the game terminology of "sweep."

HOW TO PLAY

This game doesn't use all of the cards. Remove all of the 8s, 9s, and 10s, and set them aside. Aces are low.

♦ **ACE:** 1 point

♦ **NUMBER CARDS (2 THROUGH 7):** Points equal the value of their ranks. For example, 2s are worth 2 points, 3s are worth 3 points, and so on.

♦ **JACK:** 8 points

♦ **QUEEN:** 9 points

♦ **KING:** 10 points

Deal three cards to each player, and four faceup in a row on the table. These cards are called the "layout."

Players now take turns trying to capture layout cards. A player plays one card from his hand faceup on the table, and, if he is able, uses one of three capturing methods: matching cards, adding up cards, or both.

♦ **MATCHING:** If the player's card has the same rank as one of the layout cards, he captures it.

For example, if the 2 of hearts is among the layout cards, and a player plays the 2 of clubs, he captures the 2 of hearts. A player's card can only capture one layout card at a time with this method. In the example above, if the 2 of hearts and the 2 of diamonds were part of the layout, and the player played the 2 of clubs, he could only capture one of the 2s from the layout.

♦ **ADDING:** If the ranks of any number of layout cards can be added up to equal the rank of the player's card, then all of those cards can be captured.

For example, if the 7 of clubs and 3 hearts are among the layout cards, and a player plays the 10 spades, she captures the 7 of clubs and the 3 hearts (because 7 + 3 = 10). In this example, the 7 of clubs and 3 hearts are called a "set."

If there is more than one set of cards on the table that add up to the value of the card played, only one set can be captured at a time. For example, among the layout cards are the 2 of hearts, 2 of diamonds, 2 of clubs, 5 of spades, and ace of diamonds. If a player plays the 6 of diamonds, she must choose to capture either the three 2s (2 + 2 + 2 = 6) or the 5 and the ace (1 + 5 = 6). Layout cards cannot be part of more than one set.

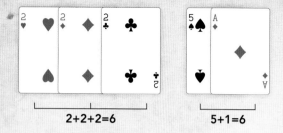

2+2+2=6   5+1=6

If a player plays a 6, she can only
capture one of the two available sets.

If a player can choose between capturing
cards by matching or by adding, he must
choose matching first. For example,
among the layout cards are the 2 of clubs,
3 of hearts, 4 of diamonds, and queen of
spades. In her hand, a player holds the
queen of hearts. During her turn, she must
use the queen of hearts to capture the
queen of spades. She could use her queen
of hearts (worth 9) to capture the 2 of
clubs, 3 of hearts, 4 of diamonds (because
2 + 3 + 4 = 9), but she also has the option
of capturing by matching her queen to the
queen of spades, so she must do that first.

When a player captures cards, he stacks
them all facedown in a pile in front of him,
and this is called his "capture" pile.

A player can only make one capture in
a turn.

If a player can't make any captures, she
must still play a card. In this case, her card
remains faceup on the table, and becomes
one of the layout cards. This is called
"trailing" a card. If a player attempts to trail
a card, but it can actually be used to make a
capture, the player must make the capture.

When a player captures all of the layout
cards in one play, it's called a "scopa," or
"sweep." He marks this by placing the card
he used to make the capture faceup in his
stack of captured cards. This will count for
extra points later on.

After all the players use up the three
cards they were originally dealt, the dealer
gives three new cards to each player, and
the game continues.

Continue playing until the deck is all
used up, and no one has any cards left
in their hands. The round ends, and any
remaining layout cards go to the player
who last made a capture, but this does not
count as a scopa.

Now players calculate their points:

♦ **MOST CARDS:** The player who
captured the most cards collects 1 point.
If it's a tie, no one wins this point.

♦ **MOST CARDS OF DIAMONDS SUIT:**
The player who captured the most cards of
the diamond suit collects 1 point. If there's
a tie, no one wins the point.

♦ **7 OF DIAMONDS (KNOWN AS THE
"SETTE BELLO," OR "BEST SEVEN"):**
The player with this card collects 1 point.

♦ **FOR EACH SCOPA:** A player collects
1 point.

♦ **ONE CARD OF EACH SUIT:** If a
player captures at least one card of each
suit, this counts as a "primiera," and it's
worth 1 point.

♦ **PRIMIERA SCORE:** If a player has
a primiera, he must then also calculate
his primiera score. The player who has
the highest primiera score collects 1
point. The primiera score is a separate
score from the player's main score for
the game, as described below.

To figure out a primiera score, a player
first selects from his captured cards
the highest-ranked card of each suit.

The player adds them together according to these rules:

- **FOR EACH 7:** Add 21 primiera points.
- **FOR EACH 6:** Add 18 primiera points.
- **FOR EACH ACE:** Add 16 primiera points.
- **FOR EACH 5:** Add 15 primiera points.
- **FOR EACH 4:** Add 14 primiera points.
- **FOR EACH 3:** Add 13 primiera points.
- **FOR EACH 2:** Add 12 primiera points.
- **FOR EACH KING, QUEEN, OR JACK:** Add 10 primiera points.

The first player to reach 11 points wins the entire game.

If there's a tie, the points earned on the most recent deal determine who wins, based first on whoever won the most cards.

If it's still a tie, then the winner is whoever won the most diamonds, then who won the sette bello, then who had the primiera, and finally, whoever won the most scopas.

SCOPONE

In this version of Scopa, two teams play against one another. Each team is made up of two players, who sit across from one another at the table.

The rules are the same except that, at the start of the game, each player is dealt ten cards facedown, and none are dealt faceup to the table. This means that the first player must trail a card.

The rules for capturing and scoring are the same. However, rather than play to 11 points, teams play to 15 points. Players combine their captured cards when figuring the score.

CHAPTER 2

SHEDDING GAMES

CHASE THE ACE

TYPE OF GAME: SHEDDING | **NUMBER OF PLAYERS:** 2 or more, up to 51

OBJECT: Trade cards to avoid holding the lowest-ranked card, and ultimately be the final player in the game

This shedding game also goes by the name of Cuckoo and (especially in Britain) Ranter Go Round.

HOW TO PLAY

Each player will need three counters. Use any small objects, such as coins or candies.

All the players should sit in a circle or around a table. Deal one card to each player, and leave the rest of the deck on the table as the stock.

Players need to avoid holding the lowest card, so the lower-ranked his card, the more a player should try to swap it. The higher-ranked his card, the more he should try to keep it. For this game, aces are low.

If a player has a king, she will want to keep it by saying "Stand."

Since aces are low, try to get rid of an ace through an "Exchange."

Each player now takes a turn, during which she has two choices: she may keep her card (if it is a king, she must show it to everyone), and she does this by saying "Stand"; or she can try to swap it with the card that the player on her left is holding, and she does this by saying "Exchange."

The player to her left can only refuse to swap if he is holding a king, in which case he must show everyone that he has a king—he must say "Cuckoo" when he does this, and after that, the next player takes his turn. If he doesn't hold a king, he must exchange his card with the player who requested the swap.

If a player requests an exchange, and the player on her left passes her an ace, 2, or 3, the player on her left must announce the rank of the card to everyone.

When it becomes the dealer's turn, he can swap his card with one drawn from the stock. If he draws a king, he loses a counter, which he must place in the center of the table, and then a new round begins. If he chooses not to exchange his card, or if he does choose to do so and doesn't draw a king, the round ends, and all the players must reveal their cards.

Whoever holds the lowest card loses a counter and places it in the center of the table. If there's a tie, all the players in the tie lose a counter. After the players figure out who loses a counter, all the cards are gathered up and a new round begins.

When a player loses all three of her counters, she is out of the game. The last player remaining wins the game.

CHEAT

TYPE OF GAME: SHEDDING

NUMBER OF PLAYERS: 3 or more (6 or more players should shuffle two decks of cards together)

OBJECT: Be the first to shed all of your cards

Another name for this popular game is I Doubt It.

HOW TO PLAY

Deal out all the cards. Some players can have a few cards more or less than others.

In a player's turn, she places one to four cards from her hand in a stack facedown on the table, starting with the lowest-ranked cards. Aces are low. All of the players will place cards on the same facedown stack, which is called the "discard pile."

The first player to take a turn must announce how many cards she's placing on the table, and that they are aces. For example, she may place a stack of cards facedown on the table and say, "Three Aces."

If two decks have been combined, a player can say he's placing up to eight cards on the table.

The next player does the same, but this player must say he's placing 2s, as in "Four 2s." The player after that must say he's placing 3s on the table, and so on, until a player announces that she's placing kings on the table.

After that, the next player starts at the beginning, announcing that he's placing aces on the table.

This is why the game is called "Cheat": for example, in a player's turn, he may announce that he's placing four 5s on the table. The truth is that he could be placing any number of cards, and none of them actually have to be 5s. Players can lie.

When a player announces what she's placing on the table, any other player can challenge her by saying "Cheat." If this happens, she must reveal the cards that she just played to the table, by turning them faceup.

If she was telling the truth, then the player who called "Cheat" must take the entire discard pile and add it to his hand. If the challenged player was lying, she adds the discard pile into her hand.

If more than one player said "Cheat," then whoever called it first is the official challenger. In a tie, the player closest to the challenged player's left side is the official challenger.

After the challenge, the next player in turn continues the game by laying down the next card that was going to be played. For example, if a player is challenged for laying down 5s, then no matter the result of the challenge, the next player lays down 6s (or says he does).

The first player to shed all of her cards wins the game, unless she is challenged in her last turn, and she loses the challenge, in which case she would have to fill her hand with the discard pile.

FAN TAN

TYPE OF GAME: SHEDDING   **NUMBER OF PLAYERS:** 3 to 8

OBJECT: Shed your cards first, and collect counters from the other players

This goes by many names, including Sevens, Parliament, Domino, and Spoof Sevens.

HOW TO PLAY

Before starting, make sure every player has the same number of counters. These can be any small items, such as coins or candies. Any number of counters can be used.

Deal all the cards. It's okay if some players have a few cards more or less than others.

The first player must play a 7 faceup on the table. If she doesn't have a 7, she pays one counter to the center of the table. This area is called the "pool."

If the first player doesn't have a 7, the next player must play a 7, and if he doesn't have one, he pays a counter to the pool.

This continues around to each player in turn, until someone plays a 7. If a player holds a 7, he must play it to start the game.

Once a 7 is on the table, each player in turn must play either the next-highest or next-lowest card, of the same suit, or another 7. If a player doesn't hold any of these cards, she must pay a counter to the pool. Aces are high.

For example, if the first card played is the 7 of clubs, the next player must play either the 6 of clubs or the 8 of clubs, or

another 7. If he doesn't have any of those cards, he pays one counter to the pool.

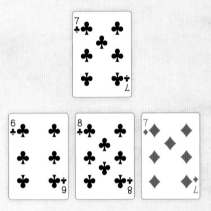

If the 7 of clubs is the faceup card, players may only play the 6 of clubs, a 7 of any suit, or the 8 of clubs.

If he has the card that's lower-ranked (in this example, it's the 6 of clubs), he places it to the left of the 7. If he holds the higher-ranked card (the 8 of clubs), he places it to the right of the 7. If he holds another 7, he places it below the 7 on the table.

As the game progresses, there will be four rows of cards on the table. Each row will have cards of the same suit, and when a row is completed it will contain thirteen cards. There will be an ace on the left side, with the cards following to the right in order ace-2-3-4-5-6-7-8-9-10-jack-queen-king.

If a player can play a card during his

turn, he must play it. If he doesn't play a card when he can, and another player calls attention to this (it usually becomes clearer what cards people are holding when there are only a few cards left in the game), he must pay three counters to each player, plus five more counters to the players holding the next highest and lowest cards of the same suit to the card he was holding and didn't play it when he had the chance.

The first player to shed all her cards collects all of the counters in the pool, and collects one counter from each player for every card they're still holding.

Whoever collects all of the counters wins the game.

◆ ◆ ◆

GO FISH

♣

TYPE OF GAME: SHEDDING   **NUMBER OF PLAYERS:** 2 to 5

OBJECT: Shed all of your cards first, and capture the most books

The origins of this game stretch back to Italy in the fifteenth century.

HOW TO PLAY

For two or three players, deal seven cards to each player. With four or five players, deal five cards to everyone.

Leave the rest of the deck facedown on the table. These cards will be the stock.

Players take turns asking for cards from other players. The goal is to collect "books" of cards. A book is all four cards of the same rank, also known as "four of a kind."

In this game, a hand of four cards of the same rank is called a "book."

When it's a player's turn, he can ask any other player for a specific card. The player who's asking must have at least one card of that rank in his hand. The player being asked must give over the card if she has it.

For example, Player 1 could ask Player 2, "Do you have the king of clubs?" Player

1 can only ask this if he has at least one king in his hand. If Player 2 has the king of clubs, she must give it to Player 1.

If this card completes a book for Player 1 (in other words, if he now has four kings), he places them faceup on the table.

During his turn, if a player asks for a card and receives it, he repeats his turn. It doesn't matter if he completes a book or not. As long as he asks for cards and receives them, his turn continues.

If a player asks another for a card, and the player being asked doesn't have that card, she must say, "Go fish." Then the player who asked for the card must draw the top card from the stock. If this card completes a book, the player places the book faceup on the table and repeats his turn.

If a player has to go fish, and he doesn't complete a book, then his turn ends, and the next player starts her turn.

The game continues until one player manages to shed all the cards in her hand, either by laying them down in books or by giving them away when asked. The first player to shed all the cards in her hand wins the game. If more than one player goes out at the same time, the winner is the one who collected the most books.

There are several variations to these rules. In the most common variation, instead of asking for a specific card using the rank and suit (such as, "Do you have the 8 of clubs?"), a player asks for all of the cards another player has in a specific rank. For example, a player would ask, "Do you have any 8s?" and the player being asked must give over all of the 8s in his hand, if he has any.

In another version, the game continues until all of the players shed their cards, and the winner is the one who collected the most books.

OLD MAID

TYPE OF GAME: SHEDDING

NUMBER OF PLAYERS: 2 or more (if there are more than 6 players, shuffle two decks together)

OBJECT: Shed pairs of cards, and avoid holding the queen (the "old maid") at the end

There are different versions of this famous game around the world. In France it's called Le Vieux Garçon, (or "the old boy") and in Germany it's called Schwarzer Peter (or "black Peter," which refers to the color of the suits involved). In the versions described here, the card to avoid is the jack of clubs, or the jack of spades, instead of a queen.

HOW TO PLAY

First, remove one queen from the deck, and set that card aside. Play the game with the remaining cards—in other words, play with a deck that has only three queens in it.

Deal out all the cards. It's okay if some players have a few cards more or less than others.

Players remove any pairs they hold, for example, two kings or two 7s, and set them aside. If a player manages to shed all his cards at this point, he is safe and can sit out the rest of the game.

In a player's turn, she offers her cards, spread out and facedown, to the player on her left. That player must take one card and add it to the cards he's holding. If that card makes a pair, he removes those cards and sets them aside with the other pairs.

Whenever a player uses up all of her cards, she is safe and can sit out for the rest of the game.

Play continues until all of the pairs have been found. The player stuck with the lone queen at the end of the game loses.

There are several variations of this game. In one popular version, players can only set aside pairs of cards that have the same-colored suit, as well as rank. For example, the 6 of diamonds and the 6 of hearts would be a pair (they're both red), but the 6 of diamonds and 6 of clubs would not count as a pair (because one is red and one is black).

PINK NINES

TYPE OF GAME: SHEDDING   **NUMBER OF PLAYERS:** 2 to 12

OBJECT: Shed all of your cards first

This game is similar to Stops.

HOW TO PLAY

Deal four cards facedown and set those cards aside. This is the "dead" hand, and won't be used for the rest of the game.

Now deal cards among the players. Everyone will need the same number of cards. When the dealer doesn't have enough cards left in the deck to make sure everyone has the same number of cards, he stops and sets the rest of the deck aside.

Each player should put her cards in order. This will help her find the cards she needs during the game. Aces are high, and the 9 of hearts and 9 of diamonds (the "pink nines") are wild. This means they can represent any card the player chooses.

The player who plays one of the "Pink Nines" can choose for the card to represent any card in the deck.

The first player starts by playing the lowest card he has. He places this card faceup on the table. If he can play more cards on top of this one, he must. To do so, he must play cards in order, so each card he plays is one rank higher than the previous card (the suit doesn't matter).

Play continues in the same way. Each card played must be ranked one higher than the previous. If a player can play a card during her turn, she must play it, and if a player can play more than one card during her turn, she must.

If every player becomes stuck, and no one can play a card, then the last player who played a card starts a new sequence by playing the lowest card he holds, and the game continues as before.

If someone plays an ace, it's called a "stop," which means that no one can play a card that's one rank higher. The person who played the ace starts a new sequence by playing the lowest card in her hand.

The first player to shed all of his cards wins the game.

SNIP SNAP SNOREM

TYPE OF GAME: SHEDDING   **NUMBER OF PLAYERS:** 3 to 8

OBJECT: Shed all of your cards first and win all the counters

This is an old variation of Fan Tan and Stops that has been written about as far back as 1782. It's also known as Earl of Coventry.

HOW TO PLAY

Deal out all the cards one at a time. Players do not have to have the same number of cards.

The first player places a card from his hand faceup on the table. The next player must play a card of the same rank or pass on his turn, and so on around the players until all four cards have been played. All four cards of one rank are called a "set."

For example, if the first player places a jack on the table. The next player must play a jack or pass, and so will the next player and the player after that. When all four jacks have been played, the set is placed in a discard pile.

The player who completes the set (the player who plays the fourth jack, in this example), then plays a new card faceup on the table, and the players must complete the new set of four cards.

When the second card of a set of four is played (in other words, when there are two cards of the same rank faceup on the table), the player must say, "Snip." When the third card is played, that player says, "Snap," and when the fourth card is played, the player says, "Snorem." The penalty for not saying the correct word at the correct time is that the player must miss a turn.

Snip!

Snap!

Snorem!

The first player to shed all of her cards wins the game.

In one popular version of this game, players start the game with the same number of counters. These can be any small items, such as coins or candies. Any number of counters can be used.

If a player can't play the required card, he must "pay" one of his counters by placing it in the center of the table. The collection of counters is called the "pool."

If the first two players make the correct

plays, the first one is "snipped" and must pay a counter to the pool.

If two or more players in a row can play cards, and the first of them played the second of the four cards, he is "snapped" and must pay two counters to the pool. If two or more players in a row can play cards, and the first of them played the third of the four cards on the table, he is "snored" and must pay three counters to the pool.

For example, in a game with three players, the table doesn't have any faceup cards on it (either because it's the start of the game or a set of four cards has just been cleared and set aside):

♦ Player A places the 3 of hearts faceup on the table.

♦ Player B must play a 3, but she doesn't have one, so she pays a counter to the pool.

♦ Player C plays the 3 of spades.

♦ Player A plays the 3 of clubs.

♦ Player B still has no 3s, and pays another counter to the pool.

♦ At this point, Player C and A were able to make two plays in a row. The first of them, Player C, had played the second card of the four needed to make the set, so that player was "snapped" and must pay two counters into the pool.

The winner of the round (the first player to shed all of his cards) wins all of the counters in the pool, along with winning one counter from each player for every card that they're still holding.

In this version, players will play several rounds, and the player who wins all of the counters from every player wins the game.

♦♦♦

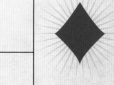

| **TYPE OF GAME:** SHEDDING | **NUMBER OF PLAYERS:** 2 to 12 |

OBJECT: Shed all of your cards first and win the most counters

This game received its name from Halley's Comet, when it appeared in 1758. The game is also an early version of Pink Nines.

HOW TO PLAY

Before starting, make sure every player has the same number of counters. These can be any small items, such as coins or candies. Any number of counters can be used.

Remove the 8 of diamonds, and set it aside for the rest of the game. Then remove the three other 8s and all of the 7s, and keep them in two separate facedown piles.

Deal out the rest of the cards in the deck. Each player should receive the same number of cards, so once the deck has run out, begin dealing out the 7s and then the other three 8s, as many as are needed to make sure everyone has the same number of cards. Set any extra 7s and 8s aside for the rest of the game.

After dealing, each player places one counter in the middle of the table. This is called the "ante," and the collection of counters is called the "kitty."

The first player starts by playing the lowest-ranked card in his hand. (Aces are high.) This is known as "leading." He places this card faceup on the table.

In turn, every player must play a card that is ranked one higher than the previous card, and of the same suit as the previous card.

If a player can play a card into this sequence, he must, and if he can play more than one card in the same turn, he must.

For example, the first player leads with the 5 of hearts. If he has the 6 of hearts, he must play it also. If not, then the next player in turn must play the 6 of hearts. If that player can't, he passes and the next player takes a turn. This continues until someone plays the 6 of hearts, which must be followed by the 7 of hearts, and so on. The game continues in this way until play become stuck, which means that no one can play the next card that's needed for the sequence, or until someone plays the 9 of diamonds.

The 9 of diamonds is a special card, known as the "Comet." If a player holds the Comet, she must play it either during her own turn or when the game is stuck. Before she plays the Comet, she must play as many cards as she holds that fit the sequence.

For example, a player holds the 4-5-6 of clubs and the Comet. The player before her plays the 3 of clubs. In her turn, she plays the 4-5-6 of clubs, and now that she can't play another card in sequence, she plays the Comet.

When someone plays the Comet, the other players each give her two counters.

After someone plays the Comet, the next player must play either the 10 of diamonds or the next card in the sequence that was being built before the Comet was played.

Whenever someone plays the king of any suit, every other player gives this player one counter.

Play continues until someone plays the ace, which ends the sequence. Whoever played the ace leads the next sequence, playing the lowest card in his hand.

The first player to run out of cards wins the round. This player wins all of the counters in the kitty, and also wins two counters from each player.

Players left holding kings when another player wins the round must give one counter to the winner for every king they're holding.

Players who run out of counters are out of the game.

The game continues until one player has won all the counters. This might take some time, so a useful option is for players to decide at the start of the game how many rounds they want to play. Once they've reached that target, then whoever won the most counters wins the game.

LEVEL: MEDIUM	CRAZY EIGHTS
TYPE OF GAME: SHEDDING	**NUMBER OF PLAYERS:** 2 to 7, or more (for 6 or more players, it's usual to combine two decks of cards)

OBJECT: Be the first to shed all of your cards and win the most points over several rounds

This incredibly popular game started off in the 1930s, when it was known as Eights. Many people have taken the basic rules and changed them over time. The most famous variation is Crazy Eights.

HOW TO PLAY

Deal five cards to each player. If there are only two players in the game, deal seven cards each. Leave the rest of the deck facedown on the table as the stock.

Turn over the top card and place it to one side. This starts the discard pile. If the top card is an 8, place it back into the middle of the deck, and use the next card to start the discard pile.

Each player takes a turn placing one card from his hand faceup onto the discard pile. He must play a card that matches either the rank or the suit of the card that's currently on the pile.

For example, if the first card on the discard pile is the 6 of clubs, then the first player must play either another 6 (such as the 6 of diamonds) or another club (such as the 2 of clubs).

If the first card on top of the discard pile is the 6 of clubs, the next player must play either another 6 or another club.

An 8 of any suit is a "wild" card, which means a player can place this card on the discard pile during her turn regardless of what rank and suit are needed.

For example, if the top card of the discard pile is the 7 of diamonds, a player would normally need to play a 7 or a diamond, but if she has an 8, she can play it on the discard pile. When a player places an 8 on the discard pile, she must choose and announce the new suit, which the next player must follow.

For example, if the top card of the discard pile is the jack of spades, and a player places the 8 of hearts on the pile, he then announces what suit the next player must follow (it doesn't need to be the same suit as the 8 she just played). If he says, "clubs," the next player must play a club.

During a player's turn, if she can't play a card to the pile (if she doesn't have any cards of the right rank or suit), or if she doesn't want to play a card from her hand (she might want to save specific cards, such as 8s, for later in the game), then she must take the top card from the stock and add it to her hand. She will have to continue taking a card from the stock until she plays a card to the discard pile, or until the stock runs out.

When the stock is used up, if a player can't play a card from his hand, or he doesn't want to give up his cards, the next player takes a turn.

The game continues until one player uses up all of the cards in her hand, or until no one can play cards to the discard pile.

If a player uses up all of her cards, she wins the round and collects points from the other players, based on the rank of the cards each player holds. For each of the following, she collects:

♦ **ACE:** 1 point

♦ **NUMBER CARD 8:** 50 points

♦ **NUMBER CARD 10, AND JACK, QUEEN, OR KING:** 10 points

♦ **NUMBER CARDS 2 THROUGH 7 AND 9:** Points equal the value of their ranks. For example, 2s are worth 2 points, 3s are worth 3 points, and so on.

If the round ends because no one can continue playing cards to the discard pile, then each player uses the scoring rules to figure out how many points the cards they're holding are worth.

The player with the lowest number of points wins the round and collects points based on the difference between the point value of her hand and the point value of every other player's hand.

For example, there are three players in the game, and the round ends because no one can play any more cards to the discard pile. All three players are still holding cards. Each player adds up the point value of the cards they're holding. Player A's cards are worth 55 points, Player B's cards are worth 70 points, and Player C's cards are worth 100 points.

In this example, Player A wins the round because his hand is worth the fewest points. From Player B, Player A collects 15 points (the difference between 70 and 55), and from Player C, he collects 45 points (the difference between 55 and 100).

Players continue to play rounds until they reach a certain number of points, usually 500, or until they've played a certain number of rounds determined at the start of the game. At that point, the player with the most points wins the game.

In some versions of this game, players collect counters rather than tally points. Counters can be any small items, such as coins or candies. Any number of counters can be used. Because the number of points a player can score is large (a hundred or more), a large number of counters will be needed for this version. The winning player in each round collects counters from the other players. When a player runs out of counters, he leaves the game. The player who wins all of the counters wins the game.

DUDAK

TYPE OF GAME: SHEDDING   **NUMBER OF PLAYERS:** 2 to 4

OBJECT: Shed all of your cards first and avoid being the last player left holding cards

This is a popular game from the Czech Republic.

HOW TO PLAY

Depending on how many players are in the game, the deck will have to be modified in different ways.

For a game with just two players, remove all of the cards ranked 2 through 8. The deck will then contain twenty-four cards (all the 9s through aces).

If there are three players, remove all of the cards ranked 2 through 6, along with two of the 7s. It doesn't matter which two 7s. They can be the two red 7s or the two black 7s, or one red 7 and one black 7. The result is a deck of thirty cards (all the 8s through aces, plus two 7s).

If there are four players, remove all of the cards ranked 2 through 6, leaving a thirty-two-card deck (all the 7s through aces).

Regardless of how many cards are in the deck, aces are high.

Deal out all of the cards in the deck.

The first player starts a discard pile by playing a card from his hand faceup on the table. After that, each player takes a turn, trying to play two cards from her hand onto the discard pile.

The first card she plays must have a higher rank than the card on top of the discard pile, and it must also be of the same suit. For example, if the card on top of the discard pile is the 7 of clubs, she must play a club ranked higher than 7, such as the 8 of clubs. If she does this, then she can play any card she chooses from her hand as her second card.

If a player can't play the first card in her turn (that is, if she doesn't have a card that's higher-ranked and of the same suit as the card on top of the discard pile), then she must take the top card from the discard pile and add it to her hand.

She continues taking cards from the top of the discard pile until she gets to a card that allows her to make her first play. If she takes all of the cards in the discard pile before this happens, then her turn ends, and the next player plays one card faceup on the table to start a new discard pile.

A player doesn't have to play the first card in her turn, even if she has a card that is higher rank than the card on top of the discard pile. She may choose to keep her card, or pick up cards from the discard pile, especially if she wants to keep strong cards in her hand.

Strong cards are highly ranked cards, or several cards that are all of the same suit. They're considered to be strong because of a special rule about "trumps" in this game.

At any point during the game, a player

has one chance to choose a suit to be his "personal trump suit" for the entire game. Cards in this suit will always be ranked higher than cards in any other suit, regardless of their rank, but only during this player's turn. If another player chooses a different suit as her personal trump, then that suit always wins for her during her turn.

For example, during her turn, a player says, "I choose diamonds to be my personal trump." The top card of the discard pile is the 10 of clubs, and in her hand she doesn't hold any clubs. She does have the 7 of diamonds, and she plays it to the discard pile. Then, for her second card, she can play any card she chooses from her hand.

A player doesn't have to choose a personal trump, but if she does, she cannot change or cancel out her choice for the rest of the game. Other players can choose the same suit to be their personal trumps, too.

If the player with the 7 of diamonds declares that diamonds are her trump suit, she may play this card as higher than the 10 of clubs.

Additionally, once a player has announced a personal trump, if he's ever in a situation where he cannot (or doesn't want to) play his first card during his turn (that is, play a card that is either in his personal trump suit, or is higher-ranked than the top card of the discard pile, and of the same suit), then rather than pick up cards one at a time from the discard pile, he must pick up the entire pile and add it to his hand. If this happens, his turn ends, and the next player starts a new discard pile with one card from her hand.

As players run out of cards, they leave the game. If a player leaves the game by playing her final two cards, then the rest of the players continue on with the game.

If she only has one card left at the start of her turn, and she gets rid of it by being able to play it as the first card in her turn, then before the game can continue, the discard pile is turned facedown and set aside for the rest of the game. The next player starts a new discard pile with a card from his hand.

The last player left holding cards loses.

Usually, in this game, players agree at the start to play a certain number of rounds to determine an overall winner. This is the player who loses the fewest number of individual rounds.

Another version states that one player becomes the winner when he is the only one who has not lost a round.

MUSTA MAIJA

TYPE OF GAME: SHEDDING   **NUMBER OF PLAYERS:** 3 to 6

OBJECT: Shed all of your cards first and avoid being the final player

This is a popular Finnish game, and its name means "Black Maria" (which refers to the queen of spades).

HOW TO PLAY

The queen of spades is a special card, and it's known as "Musta Maija" (Black Maria). The queen of spades is considered to be a separate card from all the others, and the player left holding it at the end loses. Except for this card, aces are high.

Deal six cards to each player, and leave the rest of the deck facedown on the table as the stock.

Turn over the top card, and place it faceup underneath the deck, sticking partway out so everyone can see it. This is a special card, known as the "trump" card, and its suit is especially important in this game. Its suit is called the "trump suit," and it cannot be a spade. If the card is a spade, place it back in the middle of the deck and turn over the new top card.

The first player now places one to six of his cards on the table, and they must all be of the same suit (that is, they must all be diamonds, clubs, hearts, or spades). This is called "leading the bout." He may lay down the queen of spades, either on its own or with other cards, as long as they are all spades, too.

After playing his cards, he "refills" his hand by drawing as many cards from the stock as he needs to hold six cards again.

If the first player has this hand, he would use the four diamond-suited cards to "lead the bout."

Now the next player tries to beat as many of the cards laid down by the previous player as she can. A card can be beaten by playing one that has a higher rank and is of the same suit. Or a card can be beaten by any card in the trump suit. The only exception is the queen of spades.

If the queen of spades has been played on the table, it can't be beaten, even by a trump card. But it is also powerless to beat any cards that have already been played on the table.

For example, if the trump suit is hearts, and a player places the king of diamonds on the table during his turn, then the next player can beat that card with a higher-ranked diamond (in this example the ace is the only one that's higher than a king) or by playing any heart. The 4 of hearts would beat the king of diamonds because hearts are the trump suit in this example. The queen of spades would not help the second player, in this case. If the first player had placed the queen of spades on the table, the next player would not be able to beat it because no cards can beat the queen of spades.

If a player manages to beat any of the cards played by the previous player, she sets aside all of the beaten cards, along with the cards she used to beat them, in a discard pile for the rest of the game. All players use the same discard pile.

If she leaves any faceup cards on the table because she cannot beat them, then she must pick them up and add them to her hand. If she has fewer than six cards in her hand, she refills her hand from the stock.

If a player manages to beat all of the cards played by the previous player, then after refilling her hand, she leads the next bout by playing one to six cards from her hand faceup on the table. As with the first

player, they must all be of the same suit.

A player doesn't have to beat a card just because he can. A player may choose to save strong cards for later in the game.

For example, a player may wish to keep as many trump cards as possible for the time in the game when the stock runs out. Having trump cards at that point will make it easier to shed cards because they will be able to beat most other cards.

A good strategy is for each player to keep an eye on what cards the player before them picks up. A player should try to keep cards that are higher-ranked and of the same suit as the high cards that the previous player picks up, so she can beat those cards when they are eventually played.

Once the cards in the stock are used up, players try to shed all their cards. The first player to shed all of his cards once the stock is empty is the winner, but in this game that's only the second-most important goal. Players want to avoid being the last player holding the Musta Maija because that player loses the game.

PALACE

TYPE OF GAME: SHEDDING

NUMBER OF PLAYERS: 2 to 6

OBJECT: Shed all of your cards first and avoid being the last player holding cards

This old and popular game goes by many other names, including Karma.

HOW TO PLAY

Before starting, players should find a funny hat that the loser will wear as their "Palace Crown." Also, the deck will need its jokers.

Dealing requires three steps:

♦ Deal three cards facedown in a row in front of each player.

♦ Then deal three cards faceup to each player. Arrange these so each one covers one of the facedown cards.

♦ Finally, deal three more cards facedown to each player. These will be each player's hand, and they are separate from the rows of cards dealt before.

Each player will be dealt an arrangement of cards that look like this.

Place the rest of the deck facedown on the table. This will be the stock.

Once all the cards have been dealt, a player can choose to exchange any number of cards from his hand with any of his faceup cards. He may not look at any of his facedown cards yet. Players usually want to keep high-ranked cards in their hands and exchange low-ranked ones.

Aces are high, and cards ranked 2 can either be played low or high (in which case it's ranked above the ace)—it's the player's choice (see below on how 2s are special in this game). Jokers are also used, but they have no rank (see page 48).

After players have made their exchanges (but remember, no one has to exchange cards), players begin taking turns.

The first player starts a discard pile by placing any number of cards from her hand faceup on the table. The cards must all have the same rank, such as two kings or three 7s. Then she must "refill" her hand by drawing enough cards from the stock to bring the number of cards in her hand back to three.

The other players now take turns playing one or more cards (if they play more than one, the cards must have the same rank) faceup onto the discard pile. The cards played must be of the same rank or higher than the cards played by the previous player, or they can be one of the special cards (see pages 48 and 49).

For example, if Player A played three 5s, Player B can play another 5 or any cards with a higher rank than 5, such as one or more 6s.

There are several special cards in the game that affect play:

♦ A 2 may be played on any card, and any card may be played on a 2.

♦ A 10 may be played on any card. When this happens, the player who played the 10 takes all of the cards in the discard pile and sets them aside for the rest of the round. These cards won't be used for the rest of the round. The player then takes another turn, starting a new discard pile.

♦ If a turn results in four cards of the same rank on top of the discard pile (either by playing all four cards at once or by adding to cards played by the previous player), the entire discard pile should be set aside for the rest of the round. These cards won't be used for the rest of the round. The player who played the fourth card takes another turn, starting a new discard pile.

♦ A joker may be played on any card, and this changes the direction of play. A joker can only be played alone—it may not be played in combination with other cards (that is, if a player places a joker on the table during his turn, he cannot place any other cards down). If someone plays a joker, the next player must try to beat the last card that was played before the joker.

Play continues until someone can't (or doesn't want to) play a card. A player may choose not to beat cards in order to save strong cards for later in the game. Whoever can't (or doesn't want to) make the play must pick up all the cards in the discard pile and add them to his hand. When a player does this, the turn passes to the next player, who starts a new discard pile, just like the very first player in the game.

If a player ends up with less than three cards in her hand after making a play, she must refill her hand. If there aren't enough cards left in the stock, take the amount that is left. When the stock is gone, players continue without refilling their hands.

Once players have used up all of the cards in their hands and in the stock, they may use one from the row of faceup cards dealt to them at the start of the game to play their turns. If more than one of these cards has the same rank, she can choose to play all of the cards with the same rank.

If a player cannot (or doesn't want to) play one of his faceup cards, he must add one of them to the discard pile before picking up the entire pile and using it as his new hand. A player may choose to do this if he believes the cards in the discard pile will be useful at this point to keep.

A player in this situation must use all of the cards in her hand before she can use another of her faceup cards. The next player then starts a new discard pile, and play continues.

If a player has used up all the cards in his hand, and also all of his faceup cards, he can use his row of facedown cards. These cards are played blindly (that is, the player cannot look to see what the cards are), by picking one and turning it faceup onto the discard pile. If that card isn't of the same rank or higher than the previous card played, the player must take the entire pile and use it as his new hand. As before, he must use all of the cards in his hand before he can use another facedown card. The next player then starts a new discard pile and play resumes.

A player leaves the game once she has used all of her cards, including her faceup and facedown cards. The only way this can happen is when the last facedown card is turned over, and it is either of the same rank or higher than the cards played by the previous player, or if the player is starting a new discard pile. Otherwise, she must pick up the discard pile and use it as her new hand.

Play continues as players drop out, until there is only one player left holding cards. That player loses the round and must become the dealer for the next round. That player must also wear the funny hat until someone else loses a round.

♦ ♦ ♦

MEDIUM | PITS

TYPE OF GAME: SHEDDING   **NUMBER OF PLAYERS:** Usually 4, but as many as 7

OBJECT: Shed all of your cards as quickly as possible

This game has its origins in China, and there are many variations, which became popular around the world.

HOW TO PLAY

Traditionally, instead of having one winner, or one loser, this game has four places where players can finish. These are usually positions where there are differences in status between the roles that people play.

Examples of such positions are, from highest to lowest: President, Vice-President, Governor, Mayor; or King/Queen, Prince/Princess, Duke/Duchess, Citizen; or Owner, Boss, Manager, Worker; or Principal, Vice-Principal, Teacher, Student. If there are more than four players, more positions can be invented.

Another popular way to identify positions is to have four different hats for players to wear, ranging from fancy-looking to silly-looking, or to have four different chairs for players to sit in, ranging from larger to smaller.

To make it easier to understand, this description will use first-place, second-place, third-place, and fourth-place.

This game requires a deck with two jokers in it. Deal out all the cards. It's okay if some players have more or less than others.

The first player places one to four cards

from his hand faceup on the table. This is called "leading the round." If the player leads with more than one card, then the cards must all have the same rank, such as two 5s or four kings.

After a player leads the round, the other players take their turns. In a player's turn, she can choose to play or pass.

If she chooses to play, she must play the same number of cards from her hand as the player who led the round. These cards must all have the same rank and be ranked higher than the card (or cards) played by the previous player.

Aces are high, but 2s are actually ranked as the highest card, above the aces. For example, the first player leads with a king. The next player must play an ace or a 2, which are the only cards ranked higher.

If a player leads with three jacks, for example, then the other players will each have to play three cards during their turn, if each chooses to play rather than pass. After the first player leads with the three jacks, the next player could play three queens (which are ranked higher than jacks). The player after that could play three kings (ranked higher than queens), and the player after that could play three aces (ranked higher than kings).

Jokers are wild and can represent any card the player chooses. When used to represent one card in a pair or more of matching cards, the regular card that the joker is supposed to represent will be ranked higher. For example, if a player leads with a 9-joker, and says the joker represents another 9, then the next player could play two 9s. The real 9s are ranked higher than the 9s that used a joker to represent a 9.

The round continues in this way until it happens that just one person plays and everyone else passes. Then the round ends. Whoever plays last in the round (instead of passing) gathers up all the faceup cards that were played on the table, turns them facedown, and sets them aside for the rest of the game. Then he leads the next round.

As players run out of cards, they leave the game. The first to run out of cards has the first-place position (and wears that hat, or sits in that chair, or takes that title). The next to run out of cards takes the second-place position, and so on.

The player who comes in last place gathers up all of the cards and becomes the dealer for the next game. After dealing out the cards for the next game, the dealer takes the highest-ranking card in her hand, and gives it to the player who took first-place in the previous game, and the first-place player gives the dealer (who had finished in last place in the previous game) any card from his hand that he doesn't want. The first-place player leads the first round in the new game.

MEDIUM | SIFT SMOKE

TYPE OF GAME: SHEDDING | **NUMBER OF PLAYERS:** 3 to 6

OBJECT: Be the last player holding cards

In some ways, this game is the exact opposite of Rolling Stone. Other names for this game are Lift Smoke, Linger Longer, and Last In.

HOW TO PLAY

If there are three players in the game, deal eight cards to each player. For a game with four players, deal six cards each. With five players, deal five cards each, and with six players, deal four cards to each.

In this game, the dealer should receive her cards last, and before dealing herself her final card, the dealer turns it faceup so everyone can see it. The suit of this card is important—it's known as the "trump suit." After everyone has had a chance to see it, the dealer adds the card to her hand. Leave the rest of the deck facedown on the table as the stock.

The first player places any card from his hand faceup on the table. This is called "leading."

Then the other players each take one turn playing a card from their hands faceup on the table. When everyone has taken one turn, the round ends, and it's called a "trick."

Players must try to play cards that have the same suit as the card that the first player led. If they can't, then they must play cards in the trump suit. Failing that,

they can play cards in any other suit.

After everyone has taken one turn (that is, at the end of the trick), the player who played the highest-ranked card in the suit that led the trick wins the trick. However, if someone played a card in the trump suit, the trump card always wins the trick, even if that card has a lower rank than a card in the suit that was led. If two trump cards were played in a trick, then the higher-ranked one wins. Aces are high.

For example, in a game with three players, where the trump suit is diamonds, the first player leads with the 9 of clubs. The second plays the 10 of clubs. The third player plays the 2 of diamonds. In this case, the third player wins the trick because he played a card in the trump suit, which always wins.

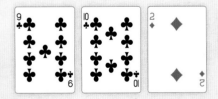

Even though the 2 has the lowest rank of these three cards, if the "trump suit" is diamonds, the 2 wins this trick.

The player who wins the trick draws the top card from the stock and adds the card to his hand. The cards that were played to the table in the previous trick are set aside. Then he leads the next trick.

As players run out of cards, they leave the game. The winner is the last player left in the game. If the last players all go out of the game in the same trick, then whoever wins that trick wins the game.

If the stock runs out before someone wins the game, then players must gather up all of the cards that were played, turn them facedown, shuffle them, and use them as the stock.

◆ ◆ ◆

LEVEL: **MEDIUM**	# SVOI KOZIRI	
TYPE OF GAME: SHEDDING	**NUMBER OF PLAYERS:** 2 to 4	
OBJECT: Shed all of your cards first		

The name of this Russian game means "one's own trumps," and it dates back to the early 1800s.

HOW TO PLAY

Before starting, players should remove all of the cards ranked 2, 3, 4, and 5 from the deck, and set them aside (they won't be used in this game), leaving a thirty-six-card deck. Aces are high.

Each player must choose one of the four suits to be his "trump suit" for the game, saying it out loud at the beginning. Everyone must have a different trump suit. Players choose in order of play.

Deal out all the cards. It's okay if some players have a few cards more or less than others. Then players must look through their hands, remove any 6s and give them to the dealer. The dealer gives one 6 to each player, in his trump suit. For example, if a player chose hearts as his trump suit, then he should receive the 6 of hearts. This ensures that each player will have at least one trump card (that is, one card in his trump suit).

While looking for 6s, player should also try to arrange their cards so they are grouped into suits. That will make it easier to play.

Players will have an easier time playing
if they group their cards by suit.

The first player places one of her cards
faceup on the table. This is called "leading,"
and it starts the "play pile" for the hand.
Each player now takes a turn, playing one
card faceup onto the play pile. On his turn,
a player has two choices: he can try to beat
the top card on the play pile by playing a
higher-ranked card of the same suit, or
he can play a card in his own trump suit
(as long as the top card of the pile is in a
different suit). It doesn't matter if the top
card is in the trump suit of the previous
player—the current player's trump suit will
always win.

For example, Player A has hearts as his
trump suit, and Player B has diamonds
as hers. At the end of Player A's turn, he
leaves the king of hearts on the play pile.
For Player B to beat this card, she could
play the ace of hearts (a higher-ranked card
of the same suit), or she could play any
diamond (which is her trump suit).

If the top card is already in the current
player's trump suit, he can only beat it by
playing a higher card in his trump suit. For

example, if his trump suit is diamonds,
and the top card on the play pile is the king
of diamonds, then the only card he could
play to beat this one would be the ace of
diamonds (it's the only card ranked higher
than the king).

If a player beats the top card on the play
pile, she leads another card right away. This
can be any card she chooses. It does not
have to be of the same suit as the previous
card, and it does not have to be able beat
the card played just before it.

A player may choose not to play a card
onto the pile. A player usually does this
if there are cards on the play pile that he
would like to have in his hand for later,
such as high-ranked cards in his trump
suit. In this case, he must pick up a certain
number of cards from the play pile and add
them to the cards in his hand:

♦ If the top card is not in the player's own
trump suit, he must pick up the top three
cards (or the entire pile, if it has less than
three cards in it).

♦ If the top card is in the player's trump
suit, and it isn't an ace, he must pick up the
top five cards.

♦ If the top card is an ace in the player's
trump suit, he must pick up the entire pile.

The player is allowed to look through
the cards in the play pile to help decide if
he wants to try to beat the top card or if
he would rather pick up cards. By looking
at the cards in the play pile, a player might
see cards that he could use to beat another
player's trump, or high-ranked cards he
could use to strengthen his own trump.

If a player chooses to pick up cards, the
next player takes a turn. If the play pile is
gone, that player starts a new play pile.

As players run out of cards, they leave the game.

If a player uses his last card to beat the top card of the play pile, and there are two or more players left in the game, the next player doesn't have to try to beat the last card. That player can lead with a new one.

The last player left holding cards loses the game and becomes the dealer for the next round. However, if the last player only has one card left, and that card beats the card on the top of the pile, the game is a draw and no one loses. In this case, the previous dealer deals over again.

♦ ♦ ♦

LEVEL: MEDIUM	SWITCH	
TYPE OF GAME: SHEDDING	**NUMBER OF PLAYERS:** 2 to 7 (for more than 6 players, it's common to combine two decks)	
OBJECT: Shed all of your cards first		

This game has many similarities to Crazy Eights. The game Uno® is based on it.

HOW TO PLAY

Deal seven cards to each player, and leave the rest of the deck facedown on the table as the stock.

The dealer turns over the top card of the stock and places it faceup next to the stock. If this card is an ace, place it back in the deck, and take the next card. This faceup card is known as the "starter."

The first player must place a card onto the starter than matches either its rank or its suit. For example, if the starter is the 5 of clubs, the first player must play either another 5 or another club.

Each player then takes a turn playing a card faceup onto the pile, and the card must match either the rank or suit of the previous card.

If a player cannot play a card, she must draw a card from the stock. If she can play that card, she must do so (and she continues drawing cards until she can't play one); otherwise she keeps the card, and the next player takes a turn.

There are several special cards:

♦ A player can play an ace, regardless of what rank or suit is called for. When an ace is played, the player must decide the suit that the next player must follow. For example, if the top card of the pile is the 8 of diamonds, a player could play the ace of spades during his turn. When he does, he can then say, "I nominate clubs." The next player must then play a club or draw a card.

Using the example given, a player can play an ace on any card of any suit. Then, she will choose what suit the ace will represent for the next player.

♦ When any 2 is played, the next player must play another 2, or else she must draw two cards from the stock and cannot play any cards to the faceup pile until her next turn (not being allowed to discard is also known as "skipping a turn").

If she does play a 2, then the player after her must play another 2 or else draw four cards and skip a turn.

If that player also plays a 2, then the next player must play a 2 or else draw six cards and skip a turn.

If that player also plays a 2, then the next player must play a 2 or draw eight cards and skip a turn.

♦ When any 4 is played, the next player must play another 4 or draw four cards from the stock and skip a turn.

If he plays a 4, the next player must play a 4 or draw eight cards and skip a turn.

If this player does play a 4, then the next must play another 4 or else draw twelve cards and skip a turn.

If that player plays a 4, then the next player must play a 4 or else draw sixteen cards from the stock and skip a turn.

♦ When any jack is played, it reverses the direction of play. The previous player must play another jack or else she skips a turn.

Except for aces, these special cards do not cancel each other out. In other words, a player cannot stop the effects of one special card by playing another. For example, if a player must play a 2, he cannot play a 4 or a jack. He could play an ace, however.

When a player has two cards left, he must announce, "Last card," when he plays one of them.

If a player makes a mistake in the rules, she must draw two cards from the stock.

The player who uses up all of his cards first wins the game.

As in Crazy Eights, a popular variation is to play for points. The winner of a game scores points based on the ranks of all the cards the other players are holding when she wins:

♦ **ACE:** 20 points

♦ **KING OR QUEEN:** 10 points

♦ **EACH 2, 4, OR JACK:** 15 points

♦ **ALL OTHER NUMBER CARDS:** Points equal the value of their ranks. For example, 3s are worth 3 points, 5s are worth 5 points, and so on.

When playing for points, it's common to play up to a certain number, usually 500. The first player to reach that amount wins the game.

DURAK

TYPE OF GAME: SHEDDING **NUMBER OF PLAYERS:** 2 to 6

OBJECT: Be the first to shed all of your cards and avoid being the "Durak" (fool)

This game is often called the most popular game in Russia. Its name translates to mean "fool."

HOW TO PLAY

There are differences when the game is played by two players, three to six players (without teams), or in teams. It's easier to understand when it's described as a game for two players first, then as a game for three to six players who aren't playing in teams, and then finally, as a game for teams to play.

Before starting, players must remove from the deck all the cards ranked 2 through 5, leaving a deck that contains thirty-six cards. Aces are high.

In a game for two players, deal six cards to each player. Leave the rest of the deck facedown on the table as the stock.

Turn over the top card and place it faceup on the table. This is the "trump" card, and its suit is the "trump" suit. Place the stock facedown on top of the trump card, leaving part of the card showing.

Each round is known as a "bout," and in each bout, one player "attacks" while the other player "defends." The attacker in the first bout is whoever wasn't dealing the cards. The winner of each bout is the attacker in the next bout.

Hearts are the "trump" suit because the faceup card at the bottom of the deck is of that suit.

A bout has two main sections, one for the attacker, and one for the defender:

♦ **ATTACKER:** The attacker plays a card from her hand faceup on the table. This first step is called "leading" a card. She can lead with any card she chooses.

♦ **DEFENDER:** The defender has two choices: pick up the card led by the attacker, adding it to his hand, or beat the card by placing another card faceup on top of it.

If the attacker's card is not in the trump suit, then the defender can beat the attacker's card by playing a card ranked higher and of the same suit. He can also beat the attacker's card by playing any card in the trump suit.

For example, if the trump card is the 10 of diamonds, the trump suit is diamonds. If the attacker leads with the 8 of clubs, the defender can beat that card if she holds any of the following cards: the 9-10-jack-queen-king-ace of clubs. They are all ranked higher than the 8, and they have the same suit. The defender can also beat the attacker's card if she plays the 6 of diamonds, for example, because diamonds are the trump suit.

If the attacker's card is in the trump suit, then the defender can only beat it by playing a higher-ranked card in the trump suit. For example, if the trump suit is spades, and the attacker leads with the king of spades, then the defender can only beat the card if he holds the ace of spades.

After the first round of attack and defense, the attacker then plays another card from her hand faceup on the table, and she places this card on top of the cards that have already been played. The attacker can only play a card that matches the rank of any of the cards played so far. For example, if at this point the faceup stack of cards on the table contains a 9 of hearts and a 10 of hearts, the attacker can only play another 9 or 10.

If the attacker is able to play another card, then as before, the defender either plays a card from his hand that will beat the attacker's card, or he picks up all of the faceup cards played so far and adds them to his hand.

If an attacker is unable to play another card, then the bout ends. The attacker turns all of the cards played so far facedown and sets them aside. These cards won't be used for the rest of the game. The attacker then becomes the defender for the next bout, and the player who had been the defender becomes the new attacker.

During attack and defense, the defender doesn't have to beat the attacker's card, even if he's holding a card that can do it. The defender may choose to pick up cards,

usually if he's holding a strong card that he wants to save for later in the game.

Whenever the defender chooses to pick up cards, the defender loses the bout, and the attacker can force him to take more of her cards. She can give him cards from her hand, as long as they match the ranks of any cards that the defender is picking up. She cannot give him more than six cards, including the ones he's picking up.

For example, the trump suit is hearts, and the attacker leads with the 10 of hearts. The defender doesn't hold any cards that can beat the 10 of hearts, so he chooses to pick up the card. At this point, the attacker can give up any other 10s that she holds.

In this example, if the defender beats her card by playing the jack of hearts, then the attacker would play another card. Remember the attacker can only play a card that matches the rank of any of the cards played so far in this round, meaning a 10 or a jack, in this example. If she plays the jack of diamonds, and the defender doesn't have any cards that can beat that, he must pick up all of the cards played so far: the 10 of hearts, jack of hearts, and jack of diamonds.

Because the defender is picking up three cards, the attacker can force him to take three more cards (she can't make him take more than six cards at once like this), as long as she gives him cards that match the ranks of cards that he's picking up. She could give him any 10 or jack that she holds.

If both players manage to keep playing until they run out of cards (that is, as long as the attacker continues to play the correct card, and the defender manages to keep beating the attacker's cards), then both players draw six new cards from the stock, and they continue the bout.

When a defender chooses to pick up the cards, or when the attacker cannot play the required card, then the bout ends. Before a new bout begins, and as long as there are still cards remaining in the stock, each player draws as many cards as he needs to bring the number of cards he holds back up to six. If a player already holds more than six cards, he won't need to draw any from the stock at this point.

If the stock runs out while a player does this, then the players begin the next bout with as many cards as they are holding—when drawing at this point, players do not take the trump card.

Once the stock runs out (remember to leave the trump card), players continue with their bouts until one player runs out of cards.

The first player to run out of cards wins the game, although, in Durak it's really more important not to be the last player left with cards. That player is called the durak, or the fool.

If the game comes down to each player holding just one card, and the defender's card beats the attacker's card, then the game ends in a tie.

When there are three to six players, who play individually (not in teams), then the rules change slightly:

♦ Deal six cards to each player. If there are six players, there will be no stock, and the last card left after dealing will be the trump card. Place this card faceup on the table.

♦ In the very first bout after dealing, the first player is the first attacker, a role that is called the "main attacker."

♦ The next player is the "first defender."

♦ The player after that is the "secondary attacker."

♦ The main attacker is allowed to ask if the secondary attacker is holding a good attacking card, meaning a high-ranked card, and especially one in the trump suit. The main attacker might ask this if she isn't holding high-ranked cards.

The secondary attacker can only say yes or no, and neither player can specify exactly what card the secondary attacker is holding. However, as a game goes on, players will notice which cards have been played already and may be able to guess at what cards other players may be holding.

♦ The secondary attacker cannot attack unless he first asks the main attacker for permission, and the main attacker says yes.

♦ In a bout, the main attacker plays as described in the two-player game. With a secondary attacker available, the main attacker may decide to let the secondary attacker play a card instead.

♦ Regardless of who attacks, the rule remains that an attacker's card (after the first card has been played) must match the rank of one of the cards that has been played in the bout already (in other words, any attack cards after the first one must match the rank of any faceup cards on the table).

♦ The attackers cannot make more than six attacks in one bout, or they cannot make more attacks in one bout than the number of cards the defender holds at the start of the bout—whichever number is lower.

For example, if a defender holds seven cards at the start of a bout, then the attackers cannot make more than six attacks in total. If a defender holds five cards at the start of a bout, then there cannot be more than five attacks in that bout.

♦ If the defender manages to beat all of the attacks in a bout, and the attackers cannot continue, then the defender wins the bout.

♦ If the defender beats six attacks, he wins the bout.

♦ If the defender starts a bout with less than six cards in his hand, and he beats all the attacks until he runs out of cards, then he wins the bout.

♦ When a defender wins a bout, all of the cards played are turned facedown and set aside for the rest of the game. The player who had been the defender now becomes the main attacker for the next bout.

♦ If a defender cannot play a card that beats an attack card, then he loses the bout. He picks up all of the cards played in the bout and adds them to his hand.

The main and secondary attacker may also force him to take cards from their hands that match the ranks of any cards played in the bout. The defender remains the defender for the next bout.

♦ Before starting a new bout, all of the players refill their hands by drawing from the stock, if there is one (remember, with six players there won't be any cards left after dealing to form a stock). The main attacker draws first, followed by the secondary attacker, and then the new defender.

♦ Once the stock is empty, players leave the game as they run out of cards in their hands. The first player to run out of cards wins the game, but as in the version for two players, it's more important not to be the last player left holding cards. That player is the durak/fool.

When playing with four or six players, Durak can also be played in teams. With four players, it can be played by two teams of two players each. Six players can play in two teams of three. In team play, opposing teams sit opposite one another at the table.

The rules for team play are the same as described in the version for two players, except that teammates cannot attack each other. In team play, a player from one team is the defender, while a member of the other team is the attacker. When a player runs out of cards, one of her teammates steps in to take her place. The first team to run out of cards wins the game, and the other team members are the duraks/fools.

PISHE PASHA

TYPE OF GAME: SHEDDING	NUMBER OF PLAYERS: 2 (or 3, for the more complicated version)

OBJECT: Shed all of your cards while also winning the most cards

Other spellings for the name of this game are Pisha Pasha and Pish Paysha, and it's also sometimes called Persian Pasha.

HOW TO PLAY

There are two versions of this game. One is very simple and fast, while the other is a little more complicated.

Here's how to play the simple version:

♦ Each player receives exactly half of the deck (twenty-six cards) as his stock. Aces are high.

♦ Players keep their cards facedown in a stack on the table, and they cannot look to see what cards they have.

♦ At the same time, each player turns over the top card from her stock and places it faceup on the table.

♦ If the two faceup cards are in different suits, then players leave the faceup cards on the table.

♦ This continues, with each new faceup card being piled up on the previous one, until players turn over two cards that are of the same suit, such as two diamonds.

♦ When both cards are of the same suit, then the player with the higher-ranked card

wins all of the other player's faceup cards and sets them aside.

Since the 7 has a higher rank, the player who played the 7 wins the cards from both stacks.

♦ When players run out of cards, whoever won the most cards wins the game.

Here's the more complicated version, which can be played by three players.

For the two-player game, each player receives exactly half of the deck (twenty-six cards) as her stock. Aces are high. Players keep their cards face down in a stack on the table, and they cannot look to see what cards they have.

The goal is to shed cards from the stock. There are two ways to do this:

♦ **FOUNDATION PILES:** Play cards onto stacks called "foundation piles." These are piles of cards that are built up in order, starting with an ace, followed by 2-3-4, and so on, up to the jack-queen-king, all of the same suit.

◆ **DISCARD PILES:** Play cards onto the other player's "discard pile." After the dealer distributes the cards, the other player turns over the top card of his stock. If it is any card other than an ace, he must discard it by placing it faceup to one side. This will start his discard pile. If it is an ace, he must use it to start a foundation pile by placing it faceup between the players.

The player should then turn over the next card in his stock. If he can play this card on a foundation pile, he must do so. This means it would either be another ace, which he would use to start a new foundation pile, or it would be a 2 of the same suit as the ace that was used to start the first foundation pile.

If this card is used to start or add to a foundation pile, the player may continue turning over the top card in his stock pile until he finds a card that he can't use in a foundation pile. That card should be placed faceup to one side to start his discard pile.

Now it's the dealer's turn. The dealer turns over the top card of her stock. If she can use it to start a foundation pile, or if she can play it on one of the foundation piles that already exists, she must do so. If the card's value is one higher or one lower than the top card in her opponent's discard pile (the suit doesn't matter), she may add it there.

As before, she continues turning over the top card of her stock until she reaches a card that she can't play on a foundation pile or onto her opponent's discard pile. She must then place that card faceup to one side, starting her own discard pile.

The other player now takes his turn. From this point on, players also have the option of using their own discard piles.

Before a player turns over the top card of his stock, he should check the top card of his discard pile. If the top card of his discard pile can be played onto a foundation pile, then he must do so.

If the top card of his discard pile fits onto his opponent's discard pile, it's up to the player to decide if he wants to play it there. A player might choose not to play a card from his discard pile onto the opponent's discard pile if he believes that card could be useful for another play later in the game, for example, if that card is close to being able to complete one of his own foundation piles.

If a player cannot play the top card of her discard pile (or if she chooses not to), she turns over the top card of her stock and plays that card as usual (either on a foundation pile, on her opponent's discard pile, or on her own discard pile).

If the opportunity arises at some point during his turn to play the top card from his discard pile, a player may do so. In other words, his turn continues as long as he can play cards either from his discard pile or from his stock.

A player's turn ends when she turns over a card from her stock that doesn't fit on a foundation pile or on her opponent's discard pile (or if she chooses not to play it there). The player must place this card faceup on her discard pile, ending her turn.

If a player breaks the rules, or makes a mistake in the game, the other player can call "stop" to point it out. If an opponent calls stop, he has two choices. He can choose either to make his opponent do the correct play or end his turn.

The mistake that happens most often (it's the easiest to make) is that a player doesn't see that the top card of her discard pile can be played on a foundation pile.

Another common error is for someone to play a card from the stock onto an opponent's discard pile, rather than on a foundation pile.

If a player places a card on his own discard pile that he could have played on his opponent's discard pile, he may not move it afterward. If a player turns over the top card of his stock, he must make use of it (playing it somewhere) before he can move any cards from his discard pile onto his opponent's pile.

When a player has used up all the cards in his stock, he turns the cards in his discard pile facedown to make a new stock.

The first player to use all the cards in his stock and discard pile wins the game. To play several rounds, keep points after each one, where the winner scores one point for each card left in the other player's stock and discard pile.

Here are some useful strategy tips:

♦ **HIGHEST RANKED CARDS:** Always try to play the highest-ranked cards on your opponent's discard pile. By placing highly ranked cards on your opponent's discard pile it becomes more difficult for him to shed those cards.

♦ **SHED KINGS:** It's especially difficult to be left with kings in the stock, so players should try to shed those when they can. Kings are always the finals cards in the foundation piles, so players must wait until the pile has been built up to that point before they can play the king.

VARIATION FOR THREE PLAYERS

Here's how to play Pishe Pasha with three players:

Deal each player seventeen cards. Then deal one card faceup in the middle of the table to start a foundation pile—there's only one foundation pile in this version of the game.

This pile begins with the value of the first card, and suit doesn't matter. Build up cards until the king is reached, then play an ace on that, followed by a 2, 3, and so on.

Everything else is the same as the two-player version above.

LEVEL: HARD | STOPS

TYPE OF GAME: SHEDDING	**NUMBER OF PLAYERS:** 4 to 8

OBJECT: Shed all of your cards first and collect the most counters

---

This old and popular game has its origins in France and England. There are so many variations that Stops is often referred to as a "family" of games that includes Newmarket, Boodle, Michigan, Chicago, Saratoga, and others.

HOW TO PLAY

This is a basic version of Stops. There are many variations, but all follow the same basic pattern of play:

♦ Players build a pile of cards in order of rank.

♦ Rather than taking turns in order, each card is added to the pile by whichever player happens to hold the card needed at that point.

♦ Some cards are not dealt to the players, which causes a "stop" to happen because no one has the specific card needed to continue building the pile.

♦ Some cards allow the players to win a number of counters at various points in the game.

Every player starts with the same number of counters. Any small items, such as coins or candies, will do. Any number of

counters can be used. For this game, twenty to thirty counters each is a good amount.

Two decks of cards will be needed for this game. From one, remove the ace of hearts, king of clubs, queen of diamonds, and jack of spades, and place them faceup on the table. They should be separate from one another and not overlapping. They can be laid out in a row, a square, or any shape players choose. These cards form what is called a "staking layout." They are also known as the "boodle" cards, and the "money" cards. Leave the rest of that deck aside. It won't be used for the rest of the game.

These four cards are known as
the "staking layout," the "boodle"
cards, or the "money" cards.

At the start of each round, before players are dealt their cards, each player places one counter on each of the boodle cards. This is known as a "stake" or an "ante" (pronounced an-tee).

Players can also choose to increase the stake to more than one counter, or to increase the stake after each round. This is a rule that players can decide on at the start of the game—whatever choice players make, each player must stake the same number of counters to the each of the boodle cards before the deal.

Now players use the other deck of cards (the one that hasn't had cards removed to form the staking layout). Deal out all of the cards, but deal as if there's one more player than there is. This extra hand of cards is called the "dead" hand, and it should be set off to one side, away from the other players. It's okay if some players have a few cards more or less than others.

Each player now looks at his hand and has one chance to exchange his hand for the dead hand. The first player who has the choice is the dealer. He can do this by announcing it and then exchanging the hands.

If the dealer doesn't want to make the exchange, then the choice goes to the player on the dealer's left, then the next player after that, and so on. If any player other than the dealer wants to exchange her cards for the dead hand, that player must "pay" a number of counters. This amount must be decided at the start of the game. For example, players may decide that it will cost three counters to "buy" the dead hand.

The counters used to buy the hand are placed in a pile on the table (it can be right in the middle of the table, or off to one side). The collection of counters is called the "kitty."

As soon as one player buys the dead hand, the opportunity to exchange hands ends until the next round. If a player buys the dead hand, or if every player refuses to buy it, then the first player (the player on the dealer's left) plays a card from his hand faceup on the table. This is called "leading," and when the player places his card on the table, he announces its rank and suit.

After the first card has been led, then whoever has the next highest card of the same suit lays it faceup on the table. This starts a "sequence" of cards. Aces are high. Players don't go in any particular order. Whoever has the right card plays it immediately.

If a player manages to play a card that matches one of the boodle cards (that is, he plays the exact same card—same rank and suit), then he wins all of the counters on that card. This does not stop the sequence, however. After the player collects his counters, the next card in the sequence must be played by whoever has it.

Players continue building this sequence of cards until it stops, either by reaching the highest-ranked card in the suit (which is the ace) or because the next card needed in a sequence is not held by any player (this means the card is in the dead hand).

When a sequence stops, then the player who played the last card before the stop must lead a new card from her hand. This begins a new sequence. The new card must be in a different suit from the one that was stopped, and it must be the lowest-ranked card the player holds in that suit. If she doesn't hold cards in any other suit, then the player to her left must lead a card to start the next sequence.

The first player to run out of cards wins the round and collects one counter from each player for every card they're still holding. He also wins all the counters in the kitty.

To start the next round, the player to

the left of the dealer becomes the new dealer. This player gathers up all of the cards, including the dead hand.

Then each player places a counter onto each of the boodle cards—any counters left from the previous round stay on the boodle cards, and new counters are added to them.

As before, the dealer deals out all of the cards, including a dead hand.

As players run out of counters, they leave the game. The game continues until there's just one player left with counters.

In some versions, players also agree at the start how many rounds they will play, and if more than one player still has counters after that number of rounds, then whoever won the majority of rounds, and still has counters, wins the game.

♦ ♦ ♦

LEVEL:
HARD

TIEN LEN

♠

TYPE OF GAME: SHEDDING | **NUMBER OF PLAYERS:** 4

OBJECT: Shed your cards and avoid being the last player left holding cards

This is one of the most popular games in Vietnam (its name is sometimes spelled Tieng Len, which is translated as "speak up" or "go forward"). An English name for it is Up the Hill.

HOW TO PLAY

Deal out all of the cards. Each player should receive thirteen cards. In the first round, the player who receives the 3 of spades takes the first turn. This is known as "leading" the round and for every round after this one, the winner of the previous round leads.

The first player in round one leads by playing the 3 of spades faceup on the table. He leads this card alone and cannot play another other cards in combination with it.

Aces are high, but, for this game, 2s are actually ranked as the highest card, above the aces. There is also an order to the suits: hearts are the highest, followed by diamonds, clubs, and then spades.

The rank is more important than the suit. For example, the 7 of diamonds is higher than the 7 of spades, but the king of spades is higher than the 5 of hearts.

After the first round, the player who leads can play one of these combinations:

♦ A SINGLE CARD

♦ A PAIR: Two cards with the same rank, such as two jacks.

♦ A TRIPLE (ALSO KNOWN AS A "TRIPLET," OR "THREE OF A KIND"): Three cards of the same rank, such as three aces.

♦ A QUADRUPLE (ALSO KNOWN AS A "QUARTET," OR "FOUR OF A KIND"): Four cards of the same rank, such as four queens.

♦ A SEQUENCE: Three or more cards in rank-order, such as 6-7-8. The cards don't have to be of the same suit. A sequence can't go past the high or low ends of the rank-order.

For example, the sequence ace-2-3 is not allowed because it would wrap around the end of the rank-order—that is, 3s are the lowest, and 2s are the highest.

♦ A DOUBLE SEQUENCE: Three or more pairs of cards in rank-order, such as 4-4-5-5-6-6. The cards don't have to be of the same suits.

An example of a double sequence.

After the first player leads (either with the 3 of spades, if he's the first player in the first round, or with one of those combinations if he's the first player in any other round), each player takes a turn.

In a player's turn, she must choose to pass or play:

♦ PASS: If she chooses to pass, it means she doesn't play any cards, and the next player takes a turn. If a player passes once, she must continue to pass for the rest of the round. That means she must wait until the next deal before she can play again.

♦ PLAY: If she chooses to play, she must play the same number of cards as were led. She must also play the same kind of combination, if a combination led the round. And finally, the card (or cards) she plays in her turn must "beat" the cards played by the previous player. Her cards "beat" another's if they are ranked higher.

For example, the first player leads with the 3 of spades. The next player must play a single card, and it must be ranked higher than the 3 of spades. She could play a card with a higher number-rank, such as the 4 of any suit. Or, she could play another 3, in a suit that's ranked higher than spades, such as the 3 of clubs.

The same rule applies if the first player leads with a combination, such as a four-card sequence made up of the 8 of hearts, 9 of spades, 10 of diamonds and jack of diamonds.

In this example, the next player would have to play another sequence made up of four cards. Her sequence could have a higher rank-order, such as the 9-10-jack-queen (the suits wouldn't matter in this case). Or, she could play a sequence with the same rank-order as the previous player's combination, but one where the highest-ranked card is in a higher-ranked suit.

For example, a sequence made up of the 8 of clubs, 9 of diamonds, 10 of clubs, and jack of diamonds would be beaten by a combination made up of the 8 of hearts,

9 of spades, 10 of diamonds, and jack of hearts—the highest-ranking card in each sequence is a jack, but hearts are ranked higher than diamonds.

To complicate things a little more (these are the sorts of rules that can make games extra-fun, with everyone trying to keep track of all the rules), there are four exceptions to these rules. These are the situations where players don't have to play a combination that matches the one that led a round, and they all involve 2s:

♦ **A SINGLE 2:** Can be beaten by any quadruple, by a 2 in a higher-ranked suit, and by any sequence of three pairs, such as 4-4-5-5-6-6.

♦ **A PAIR OF 2S:** Can be beaten by any sequence of four pairs, such as 8-8-9-9-10-10-jack-jack. Another pair of 2s can also beat them if one of the 2s has a higher-ranked suit than the 2s in the other pair. For example, a pair made up of the 2 of diamonds and 2 of clubs can be beaten by a pair made up of the 2 of hearts and 2 of spades, because hearts is the highest-ranking suit.

♦ **A TRIPLE OF 2S:** Can be beaten by any sequence of five pairs, such as 4-4-5-5-6-6-7-7-8-8.

Play continues around the table until someone plays a combination that no one else can beat. This player wins the round.

All the cards that were played must be set off to one side for the rest of the game, and the winner of the round leads off the next round with any combination.

As players run out of cards, they must leave the game. The other players continue until there's only one player left with cards.

The first to leave the game is the winner, but it's much more important in this game to avoid being the last player left holding cards. This player is the loser.

ZHENG SHANGZOU

OBJECT: Shed all of your cards and be the first to collect 11 points

This game comes from China, and its name means "struggling upstream." It's a bit of a mixture of Whist and Rummy, and it's similar to Tien Len.

HOW TO PLAY

Players will need a deck with two jokers. Make sure the jokers are different from each other, so players can tell them apart. The two jokers are called the "red joker" and "black joker." Aces are high, but 2s are ranked above aces. The black joker is ranked higher than 2s, while the red joker is the highest card of all.

Deal out all the cards. It's okay if some players have a few cards more or less than others.

The player who makes the first move in a round is the "leader." The leader must play one of these combinations to start the round:

♦ **A SINGLE CARD**

♦ **TWO TO FOUR CARDS THAT HAVE THE SAME RANK:** Such as two kings. The 2s and jokers are "wild," which means that they can be used to represent any card from 3 up to ace.

In this game, two kings together can be equal to two 2s or two jokers, because 2s and jokers are "wild."

♦ **A "SINGLE SEQUENCE":** Of three or more cards in order, such as 4-5-6. The cards don't have to be of the same suit. The 2s cannot be used in a single sequence. Jokers may be used as wild cards in a single sequence and can represent any card from 3s up to aces.

♦ **A "MULTIPLE SEQUENCE":** Of six or more cards, where cards are in order (with at least three ranks in the series) and there are two or more of each card in the sequence, such as 3-3-4-4-5-5, or 7-7-7-7-8-8-8-8-9-9-9-9-10-10-10-10-jack-jack-jack-jack. For example, a sequence of 7-7-8-8 would not be allowed because there are only two ranks in the series.

Jokers and 2s may both be used as wild cards in a multiple sequence, but 2s may not be used to represent all of the cards of a particular value. For example, the sequence 5-5-2-2-7-7 is not allowed because the 2s are representing all of the 6s. However, jokers may be used to represent any or all of the cards of a particular value. So the sequence 5-5-joker-joker-7-7 is valid, as well as 5-5-2-joker-7-7.

After someone leads the round, play moves to each player in turn. When it's a player's turn, she must pass or play.

Passing means that she doesn't play any cards and the next player takes a turn. If a player passes, she's still able to play later in the round, on her next turn.

If the player decides to play, she must follow two rules:

♦ **FIRST RULE:** Her combination must be the same kind as the one that led (that is, it must have the same number of cards in it and use the same type of combination).

For example, if a player leads with a single card, then anyone who chooses to play must also play a single card. If a player leads with four cards of the same rank, than anyone choosing to play that round must also play four cards of the same rank. If a player leads with a single or multiple sequence, then anyone wanting to play that round must play a single or multiple sequence too (that it, it must match the leader's play, in terms of type of combination and total number of cards).

♦ **SECOND RULE:** Her combination must also "beat" the previous one played.

A card, or combination of cards, beats another according to these rules:

♦ **A SINGLE CARD:** This can be beaten by another single card that has a higher rank. The suit doesn't matter. For example, a 5 can be beaten by a 6. A 2 can only be beaten by a joker. The black joker can only be beaten by the red joker.

♦ **TWO CARDS OF THE SAME RANK:** These can only be beaten by two cards

of a higher rank. For example, two 4s can be beaten by two 5s. Two jokers are the highest combination of this sort and cannot be beaten.

If a combination contains a wild card, it can be beaten by a combination with the same rank, but containing no wild cards (a combination with wild cards is called "impure," while one with no wild cards is called "pure"). For example, if someone plays two jacks, made up of the jack of hearts and the red joker, it can be beaten by two jacks, made up of the jack of spades and the jack of diamonds.

♦ **THREE CARDS OF THE SAME RANK:** These can only be beaten by three cards of a higher rank, and four cards of the same rank can only be beaten by four cards of a higher rank.

If a three-card play includes two wild cards, the player must state whether the combination is meant to be three cards of the same rank, or a three card sequence. For example, a combination made up of 8-joker-joker could be three 8s, or it could be a sequence such as 8-9-10. The player must announce what kind of combination he's playing.

♦ **A SINGLE SEQUENCE (SUCH AS 3-4-5 OR 7-8-9-10):** This can be beaten by another sequence containing the same number of cards, but with a higher-ranked top card. For example, the sequence 4-5-6 will beat the sequence 3-4-5 because each sequence contains the same number of cards (three), and the top card of the winning sequence (6) is higher than the top card of the other (5).

If the ranks of the top cards in two sequences of the same length are equal, then suit becomes important. A sequence with all of its cards of the same suit (this is known as a "flush") will beat any similar sequence in a mix of suits. For example, if a player leads with a sequence made up of the 3 of clubs, 4 of hearts, and 5 of spades, it can be beaten by the sequence 3-4-5 of diamonds because the sequence is all diamonds.

As before, a pure sequence also beats an impure sequence. For example, the sequence 3-4-joker, where the joker represents a 5, can be beaten by the sequence 3-4-5, because the second sequence does not contain a wild card.

♦ **A MULTIPLE SEQUENCE (SUCH AS 3-3-4-4-5-5):** This can only be beaten by a multiple sequence with the same number of cards, but with a higher ranked top card. For example, a multiple sequence such as 3-3-4-4-5-5 can be beaten by 4-4-5-5-6-6.

The rule about pure and impure sequences also applies here. For example, the sequence 5-5-6-6-7-7 can beat a sequence made up of 5-5-6-6-7-2, where the 2 represents another 7.

Play continues around the table until someone lays a combination that makes everyone else pass. That player gathers up the cards, sets them aside for the rest of the round, and then starts the next round by playing his next lead.

The first player to run out of cards wins the round, and the rest of the players must keep playing until there's only one left.

As players run out of cards, keep score as follows:

♦ The first player to run out of cards adds 2 points to her score.

♦ The second player to run out of cards adds 1 point to his score.

♦ Players who leave the game after the second player receive no points.

♦ The third player to run out of cards becomes the dealer for the next round.

♦ The last and second-to-last players to run out of cards are known as the "pit dwellers" and must give up their best cards in the next round to the winners of this hand. This means that after the cards for the next round are dealt, those two players must place the highest-ranking cards they've been dealt (suit doesn't matter) faceup on the table.

The player who placed first in the previous hand chooses one of these cards to take, and the second-place player takes the other one. Players add these cards to their hands, and then each discards one card faceup on the table. The pit-dweller who placed second-to-last has the first choice of which card to take, and the last-place player takes the last card.

The round proceeds as before, with the dealer making the first play. The first person to collect 11 points (over as many hands as it takes) wins the game.

CHAPTER 3

PATIENCE GAMES

CONCENTRATION

TYPE OF GAME: PATIENCE   **NUMBER OF PLAYERS:** 1 or more

OBJECT: Find the most pairs

This is a good game for developing memory skills—in fact, another name for this game is Memory.

HOW TO PLAY

Deal out all the cards facedown (any large flat surface will work). If the deck doesn't have any jokers, deal out all of the cards facedown in four rows of thirteen cards each. If the deck contains the two jokers, deal out the deck in six rows of nine cards each.

Taking turns, each player flips over any two cards. If the cards have the same rank (such as two kings) and the same color suit (hearts and diamonds are both red, while spades and clubs are both black), that player takes the cards off the table, sets them aside to start a "win" pile for himself, and takes another turn.

If the cards don't match, the player turns them facedown and returns them to where they were on the table. Then the next player takes a turn.

The player who has the most pairs when all the cards have been taken wins the game.

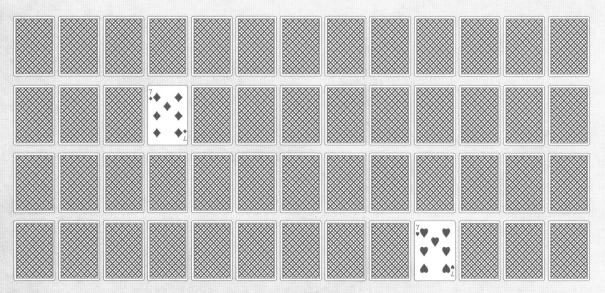

If a player turns over two cards that happen to be of the same rank
and the same color suit, the player puts them in her "win" pile.

DICTATION

TYPE OF GAME: PATIENCE

NUMBER OF PLAYERS: 2 or more

OBJECT: Complete the most sequences and collect the most points

This game can incorporate almost any version of Solitaire, which is a name that refers to games that one person can play. This description uses a game known as Sir Tommy, but another can be substituted.

HOW TO PLAY

Each player will need his own deck of cards. Pick one player to be the "dictator." This can be done any way players choose. For example, each player could pick a facedown card from his own deck, and whoever chooses the highest-ranked card becomes the dictator. Aces are low.

The dictator keeps her deck facedown on the table, but the other players keep theirs faceup. Players can spread their cards out, so they can see all of their cards and find specific cards quickly.

For each step in the game, the dictator turns over the top card of his deck and places it faceup on the table. He announces the rank and suit of the card. Every player must find that same card in his own deck.

Once each player has the same starting card, she must decide whether to play the card (which means, use it to play their own independent game—the game described here is called "Sir Tommy") or place it faceup in a discard pile. Each player will keep her own discard pile. After everyone has made their move in their own game, they let the dictator know.

When everyone's ready for a new card, the dictator turns over the top card from his deck and announces it. Everyone finds that card in his own deck and continues with his own independent game.

In order to play a card, a player first needs to have an ace. Until one turns up, a player takes from his deck each card the dictator announces and places it faceup on top of his own discard pile. Each player can create up to four discard piles and can arrange the cards in them into overlapping columns, in order to see every card in the pile. Cards in a player's discard piles cannot be moved from pile to pile, and each new card must be added to the top of the pile (it cannot be inserted into the middle of a pile).

Once an ace turns up, a player leaves it faceup in front of him. Now the player's goal becomes to build a sequence in ascending order on top of the ace (suits don't matter). The next card would have to be a 2, then 3-4-5-6-7 and so on, all the way up to a king.

A player cannot begin building until he has obtained an ace to start his sequence.

A player can use the card that was just announced by the dictator, or she may use top cards from her discard piles (the top cards are the cards that were added most recently to the pile). Either way, when a player has a card that can be played in the sequence, she can choose to play it or not. She might choose not to play it if she wants to keep cards for later. For example, she may start building cards in sequence in her discard piles, so that when the opportunity comes up to play them, she plays from them one card after another, rather than waiting for the dictator to call the cards she needs.

When all four aces eventually turn up, each player will be working on four sequences, one for each ace. A player cannot move cards from inside one sequence to another, but he can take the top card of a sequence (the card that was added most recently to a sequence) to use on another.

When the dictator has announced all of the cards in his deck, each player continues with his own game, trying to build sequences as far as she can go by using the top cards from her discard piles.

When everyone has played as far as they can, the player who has completed the most sequences completely (from ace to king) wins the game.

If there's a tie, or if no players have managed to complete a sequence, players can also add up points. Players can also choose to count points if they want to play several rounds. In that case, players should set a target total for the winner. For example, players could decide that the first to reach 100 points wins the game. Or they could decide to play a certain number of games, and the person with the most points after that wins the game.

To count points, players look at the top cards in the four sequences they were building. The top cards are counted in this manner:

♦ **ACE:** 1 point

♦ **NUMBER CARDS:** Points equal the value of their ranks. For example, 2s are worth 2 points, 3s are worth 3 points, and so on.

♦ **JACK:** 15 points

♦ **QUEEN:** 20 points

♦ **KING:** 25 points

For example, if a player managed to complete all four sequences, the top card of each sequence would be a king, and the player would earn 100 points (25 + 25 + 25 + 25 = 100). If a player ended his sequences with 8-9-queen-king as the top cards, he would earn 62 points (8 + 9 + 20 + 25 = 62).

MEDIUM | SPIT

TYPE OF GAME: PATIENCE　　　**NUMBER OF PLAYERS:** 2

OBJECT: Shed all of your cards as quickly as possible

The fast-paced game is also known as Speed. This game is usually learned from friends, so, as rules vary, some players may consider Spit and Speed different games. The following is the more common and widely known variation.

HOW TO PLAY

This is an unusual game because the players don't take turns. Both play at the same time, and the important part is to be the faster player. The faster a player completes each round, the fewer cards she will receive in the next round, until eventually she gets rid of all her cards and wins the game.

Start by dealing half of the deck (twenty-six cards) facedown to each player. Players cannot look to see what cards they received. Before play begins, each player now builds several facedown stacks of cards, which are known as his "layout piles." The layout contains five piles of cards in a row:

- ◆ The first pile has one card.
- ◆ The second pile has two cards.
- ◆ The third has three cards.
- ◆ The fourth has four cards.
- ◆ The fifth has five cards.

Each player turns over the top card of each layout pile and places it faceup back on the pile. After building the layout piles, each player now has eleven cards left in his hand. These are called "spit cards," and they must stay facedown. Players still cannot look through them to see what cards they hold.

This should be the layout for each player when the game begins.

At the same time, both players say "spit" and turn over their top spit cards. Players place these two cards side by side, faceup between the two layouts. These two cards, and the cards that will be placed on top of them during the game, will build what's called the "spit piles."

Following the rules below, both players

place cards onto the spit piles as quickly as possible, without waiting for the other player to take a turn.

Players must try to shed all the cards in their layout by moving those cards onto the two spit piles. Each player may only use one hand (the hand that isn't holding the spit cards) to touch cards, and only one card may be moved at a time.

Here's how the cards move:

♦ Players may move the top (faceup) card from any one of their layout piles onto either spit pile. To do so, the card from the layout pile must be ranked one higher or one lower than the card on top of the spit pile. The suit doesn't matter. An ace can be either high or low and may be played on a 2 or a king.

♦ Once the top card of a layout pile has been played, turn the next card in the pile faceup.

♦ If one of the layout piles is used up, a player may move the faceup card from another layout pile into the empty space, and turn the next card in the remaining pile faceup.

♦ Players may never have more than five layout piles, but as the cards get used up, they may have fewer than five piles.

♦ If a card touches a pile, or the empty space occupied by a pile, it must go there. In other words, a player may not place a card somewhere and then change his mind.

Usually, both players will reach a point where they can no longer play. This happens most often when none of the faceup layout cards can be played onto either of the spit piles. If one player gets stuck like this, but the other can continue,

the stuck player must wait until the other also gets stuck.

When this happens, both players say "spit" again, and turn over a new spit card from the cards in their hands. These cards are placed on top of the spit piles, and play resumes.

If players reach a point where neither can make a play, and one player has no spit cards left, the other player should turn over a new spit card onto just one of the spit piles. Then both players continue.

If both players get stuck, and they have each run out of spit cards, then the player with less cards remaining in his layout takes the top card from one of his layout piles and moves it to one of the spit piles. Then both players continue the game.

When one player uses up all of the cards in her layout, both players race to choose a spit pile by covering the one they want with one hand. This is called "slapping" a pile. Players should try to take the one with the smallest number of cards. If both players choose the same pile, whoever gets there first takes it, and the other player must take the other pile.

It is important for players to keep an eye on their opponent as well as their own pile. If a player notices that his opponent is about to drop his last card, he may be able to slap a pile first.

Once piles have been chosen, players take any layout cards they have left and add them to the spit piles they just picked up. Shuffle these cards to mix them up well, and deal out new layouts, as they did at the start of the game. Once the new layouts are ready, players shout, "Spit," and play resumes.

As the game continues, one player will eventually have fewer cards than the other player. If a player has fewer than fifteen cards, she won't be able to build a complete layout. When that happens, she should build as much of the layout as she can, and both players use just one spit pile (which the other player will have to start).

At this stage, when players get stuck, the player still holding spit cards gathers up the spit pile and all the layout cards, deals a new layout for both players, and starts a new spit pile. Then both players continue.

The first player to run out of spit cards and layout cards wins the game.

◆ ◆ ◆

RACING DEMON

TYPE OF GAME: PATIENCE   **NUMBER OF PLAYERS:** 2 (usually) or more

OBJECT: Be the first to shed your cards

This is an old game that goes by many names. Racing Demon is the oldest of its names. Others are Pounce, Nertz, and Grouch. It's also a form of Double Solitaire.

HOW TO PLAY

Each player will need her own deck of cards. Each deck should have a different back, or some way to identify it from the other.

Make sure each player has enough room to build several different piles and groups of cards. This is called a "work space."

To start the game, each player deals cards onto his work space, according to these rules:

♦ Deal twelve cards facedown into a pile on the right-hand side of the work space.

♦ Deal one more card faceup on top of this pile.

This pile of cards is called the "off-pile." It's also known as the "demon" pile, the "pounce" pile, or the "nertz" pile. Whatever name is being used, this pile is what the player must use up in order to win the game. (In this description, it will be called the "demon" pile.)

If the top card of the demon pile is an ace, move the card to an area between the players' work spaces, in a place where everyone can reach it easily. This area is called the "common area."

Turn over the card that was underneath

the ace, and place this card faceup on top of the demon pile.

♦ First the player sets up the demon pile. Then he deals four cards faceup onto the work space. These cards should be to the left of the demon pile. Place them in a row, side-by-side, but not overlapping or touching. These will be the start of the player's "work" piles.

Each card that goes onto a work pile needs to leave part of the previous card showing underneath, so as the work pile grows, it should be spread out enough to see all of the cards in it. At the start, when dealing the four faceup cards that begin the work piles, make sure there's enough room for these piles to grow and spread out.

If any of the four cards that start the work piles are aces, move them to the common area, and replace them with new faceup cards from the deck. Any aces in the common area should be separate from one another. Each will be the start of a pile of cards, known as "foundation" piles.

After setting up his demon pile, and work piles, and moving any aces to the common area to start foundation piles, each player places the rest of his deck face down in his work space, wherever there is room for it. This is the player's hand.

Here's how work piles and foundation piles will be built:

♦ **WORK PILES:** A player builds work piles by placing cards onto them in a special sequence. Each card that goes onto a work pile must be ranked one less than the previous card, and it must be a different color than the previous card. Aces are low.

For example, if the first card in a work pile is the 9 of clubs (clubs are black), the player would need to place either the 8 of diamonds or the 8 of hearts on top of it (diamonds and hearts are red). The next card would have to be a black 7, a red 6, and so on. Suit doesn't matter in building work piles, just color.

Each player builds her own work piles. That is, she can only use the work piles in her own work space.

♦ **FOUNDATION PILES:** Players build foundation piles in the common area. Any player can build onto a foundation pile, even if it was started by another player. The piles are in the common area, which means they are open for any player to use.

A player builds onto a foundation pile by adding a card that must be ranked one higher than the previous card and must be of the same suit as the previous card.

All foundation piles start with an ace, so the next card will have to be the 2, then the 3, the 4, and so on all the way up to king, and all must be of the same suit. For example, if the ace that starts a foundation pile is the ace of clubs, then all of the cards in that pile must be clubs.

After all of the set-up work, the real game play begins. Everyone must be ready to go, and everyone starts playing at the same time. In this game, players don't take turns. Once players start, each races to build work and foundation piles and shed all of the cards in his demon pile.

A player begins by seeing if the top card of her demon pile fits onto any of her work piles. That is, she checks to see if the card from the demon pile is ranked one less, and has the opposite color, to the top card of any of her work piles. If it does, she moves the card to the right place and then turns the new top card of the demon pile faceup.

If the top card of a player's demon pile fits onto any foundation pile, he may also play it there. Remember, for a card to fit onto a foundation pile it must be ranked one higher than the card that is currently on top of the foundation pile, and it must be of the same suit as the card currently on top of the foundation pile.

The top card of a player's demon pile is always turned faceup. Once it is used, turn the next card faceup.

A player also checks to see if any of the cards from her work piles will fit onto one another. For example, at the start of the game, if the card of one work pile is the 6 of diamonds, and the card from another is the 5 of clubs, the player can take the 5 and place it on the 6. The 5 is ranked one less than the 6, and the 5 of clubs is the opposite color (black) from the 6 of diamonds (red).

This can also be done as a work pile grows. In this situation, a player would move all of the cards from one pile to the top of another, if they fit according to the rules. For example, one of a player's work piles contains the 10 of hearts, with the 9 of spades on top of it. Another of her work piles contains the 8 of diamonds, with the 7 of spades on top of it, and the 6 of hearts on top of that. She can take the 6-7-8 pile and place it directly on top of the 9-10 pile. The ranks and colors fit the rules.

If a work pile becomes empty (if it has been moved onto another pile), the player fills the empty space with any card he has available. He may take the top card from his demon pile and place it in the empty space, or he may move a card from the top of another work pile, or he may use the top card from his hand.

When a player gets stuck, she can start a "waste" pile. When she's unable to move cards anywhere, she deals the top three cards from her hand faceup into a single pile in her work space, creating a waste pile. Once she starts a waste pile, she may also use the top card from it to fill the space if a work pile becomes empty.

A player may also get stuck if he doesn't want to play cards where they will fit. A player might do this if he wants to save some sequences—for example, he may notice that one of his work piles contains cards that will fit very well onto a foundation pile, and he doesn't want to use them for a work pile. If the top card from his waste pile fits onto a foundation pile, or onto a work pile, he plays it there. This opens up the chance for his cards to start moving again (between work piles, from the demon pile, or onto foundation piles).

If a player becomes stuck again, she deals three more cards faceup onto the waste pile, and checks to see if the new top card of the waste pile will fit anywhere.

If a player needs to deal three cards to the waste pile, but has less than three cards in her hand, she places the remaining cards from her hand faceup onto the waste pile and continues. The next time she gets stuck, she turns the waste pile facedown, moves the top card to the bottom (this changes the order of the cards), and uses it as her hand, dealing three cards faceup to start a new waste pile.

If a player still gets stuck, he should wait and watch the other players, to see if anyone adds to a foundation pile, which might create an opening for the stuck player to start moving cards again.

If more than one person plays a card

onto a foundation pile at the same time, the first player there (the person whose card is on the bottom) gets to stay, while the other players must take their cards back. If there's a tie and no one can agree on who got there first, then all the cards in the tie can stay.

If a foundation pile is completed, containing all thirteen cards in order from ace (on the bottom of the pile) to king (on top), and all of the same suit, then the player who completed it turns the pile facedown. This shows that the pile is finished, and no more cards can be added.

When a player uses up all of the cards in her demon pile, she calls out "done" (although, when the game is called Nertz, a player would call out "Nertz!"; that word is much more fun to say).

As soon as one player calls nertz, the round ends and scoring begins—players may complete the moves they have already started, but no more moves may be made.

It's important to note that a player doesn't have to call out nertz as soon as his demon pile is gone. Instead, he may choose to continue playing in order to increase his score.

A player earns 1 point for every card she plays onto a foundation pile. To figure this out, sort out the cards in the foundation piles by their back designs. Everyone else loses 2 points for each card left in their demon piles when the player called nertz.

The round also ends if all of the players get stuck, and none of the cards left in their hands will fit anywhere. In this rare case, all players lose 2 points per card left in their demon piles.

Write everyone's score down. Then each player gathers up her cards, and a new round begins. The first player to collect 100 or more points wins the game.

RUSSIAN BANK

TYPE OF GAME: PATIENCE   **NUMBER OF PLAYERS:** 2

OBJECT: Be the first to shed your cards

This is a Solitaire-type game popular in North America, Britain, and France. Other names for it include Crapette, Stop, and Touch.

HOW TO PLAY

Each player will need his own deck of cards. Each deck should have a different back, or some way to identify it from the other.

Players sit facing each other at the table. Each player will need space on the table to place his cards, called his "work space." Each player deals cards from his deck in the following layout:

♦ Deal twelve cards facedown in a pile.

♦ Deal one card faceup on top of this pile. This pile of cards is called the "reserve" pile. Place it on the right side of the work space.

♦ Deal four cards faceup. Lay these cards out in a column above the reserve pile. None of the cards should be touching. These four cards are called the four

"houses." All eight houses together (four from each player) are the "tableau."

The two columns of cards (one for each player) should have a space between them that's at least two cards wide. In other words, two cards should be able to fit between the two sets of houses.

During the game, the players will work together to build eight more piles of cards (called "foundation piles") in this space. All eight houses in the tableau, as well as all eight foundation piles, can be used by both players.

After building the reserve, and the houses, each player will have thirty-five cards left in his deck. Place these cards facedown in pile on the left side of the work space (the top of the other player's column of houses). This pile is the player's "hand."

The player's waste pile during the game will be built in the space between her hand and her reserve pile.

The player's goal in the game is to get rid of all the cards in his hand, waste pile, and reserve pile. This is done by moving these cards onto foundation piles, onto the houses in the tableau, or by adding them to the other player's waste and reserve piles.

The player with the lowest-ranked card at the top of his reserve pile goes first. If the two cards have the same rank, compare the house cards next to the reserve piles. If those are the same, look at the next house card, and so on. Aces are low.

On her turn, the player may move one card at a time onto a house in the tableau, onto a foundation pile, or onto her opponent's waste or reserve pile. If she is unable to play her card, or she doesn't want to (in order to make a better play elsewhere or later in the game), she must place it on her waste pile, which ends her turn. Once she places a card on her waste pile, that card is no longer available for her to play in later turns, although there are exceptions to this rule.

House piles begin with the card that was dealt at the start and must be built in descending numerical order and in alternating colors. For example, if the first card in a house is a black 9, the only card that can be played there next is a red 8, followed by a black 7, and so on.

When cards are played onto a house pile, the cards must overlap so that players can see all the cards in the pile. House piles are built in rows that extend outward, away from the column of house cards. If the space occupied by a house becomes empty, the player must play an available card there, starting a new house.

Foundation piles are built in the space between the two columns of houses players create at the start. A foundation pile can only be started by an ace. Because of this, there will only be eight foundation piles over the course of the game. Once started, a foundation pile must be built is ascending numerical order and of the same suit. For example, if a foundation pile has the ace of diamonds as its first card, the only card that can be played there next is the 2 of diamonds, followed by the 3 of diamonds, and so on.

Once the king has been played on a foundation pile, the pile is complete. The player turns the king facedown to show that the pile is finished.

A player may also lay cards on his opponent's waste and reserve piles. This is called "loading" those piles. The cards played there must have the same suit as the top card, and be ranked one higher or one lower. For example, if the top card of a reserve or waste pile is the jack of clubs, the only cards that can be played there would be the 10 or queen of clubs, and if the queen is played there, then the next card must be another jack of clubs, or the king of clubs.

Only the top, faceup card on the player's reserve pile, or the cards that were most recently added to any of the eight houses, may be moved at the beginning of the player's turn.

As cards are added to the tableau, they are overlapped in a row that extends outward, away from the foundation piles. So, the most recently added card in a house is the one at the end of the row of cards (the one that isn't covered by another card).

As these cards are moved, more cards become available to be moved. When the top card from the reserve pile is played, turn the next card on that pile faceup. The new faceup card then becomes available to be moved.

When the reserve pile is empty, it remains that way for the rest of the game.

There are several rules in this game that are known as "necessary rules." Players must watch their opponent to be sure that they follow the rules:

♦ **NECESSARY RULE ONE:** If the top card on the reserve pile can be played onto a foundation pile (that is, if it fits the rules for building a foundation pile), a player must make this move before playing any other card.

♦ **NECESSARY RULE TWO:** When a card that's available to be moved can be played onto a foundation pile, it must be played. If more than one card is available to be moved onto a foundation pile (and none of them are on the reserve pile), the player may choose which card to play first.

♦ **NECESSARY RULE THREE:** If there are any empty spaces in the tableau, the player must refill them with cards from his reserve pile (if his reserve pile is not empty).

If the necessary rules are not followed, the player's opponent can call out "Stop." If a player stops someone, she has to explain what the other player did wrong.

If a card is placed somewhere incorrectly and "stop" is called, the player must undo the move and his turn ends.

If a player misses making a necessary move, and her opponent stops her, she must undo the move she made instead of the necessary move, and then make the correct move. Her turn then ends (that is, she doesn't place one of her hand cards onto her waste pile).

When there aren't any necessary moves, the player may turn over the top card from his hand. This is not necessary unless a player cannot make any other play.

If a player has run out of moves to make, she must turn over the top card from her hand. Once the top card of the hand is faceup, it becomes available to be played. Turning this card may result in new necessary moves.

If the top card of the hand is played,
the player may turn over the new top card of his hand. If he can't play the hand card anywhere, or if he chooses not to play it, he must place it on his waste pile. Once he does this, his turn ends.

When a card is placed on the waste pile, it's no longer available to be played. If, however, it's a card that has to be played somewhere because it's a necessary move, the other player may force it to be played there instead of the waste pile.

If a player doesn't have any cards left in her hand when she needs to turn the top hand card over, she must turn her waste pile facedown and place it on the left side of her work space to make it her new hand. She can then turn the top card faceup, making it available to be played.

If a player only has one card left in his hand, and he can't play it anywhere, he must place it on the waste pile to end his turn. In this case, the player should not move his waste pile over to make a new hand until his turn comes around again because his opponent can still load cards onto his waste pile.

When a player's hand, waste, and reserve piles are all empty (that is, when she has played all of her cards), then the round ends, and she wins. The player collects 30 points for winning, plus 1 point for each card left in her opponent's hand and waste piles, and 2 points for every card in her opponent's reserve pile.

If a point is reached when neither player can make any more moves, even if they still have cards left in their hands, waste, or reserve piles, the player who has the least number of cards left in those piles wins.

Calculate points for each player (1 point for each card in the other player's hand and waste piles and 2 points for each card left in his reserve pile), and subtract the lower number from the higher number. The winner receives that amount. When a game ends like this, no one receives the 30 point bonus for winning.

Divide the cards back into their original decks, shuffle, and deal out a new round.

Players often pick a finishing score before beginning (commonly 100 points). The first player to collect that many points wins the game.

♦♦♦

SPITE AND MALICE

TYPE OF GAME: PATIENCE   **NUMBER OF PLAYERS:** 2

OBJECT: Be the first to shed all of the cards in your "pay-off" pile

Another name for this game is Cat and Mouse.

HOW TO PLAY

Two decks of cards will be needed for this game. Aces are low, and kings are "wild," meaning they can represent any card.

Players should sit facing each other at a table. One player shuffles both decks together into one, and deals two piles of cards facedown, with twenty cards in each pile. These are "pay-off" piles and are placed in a column to the dealer's right. Be sure to leave space for another stack of cards between the pay-off piles.

Deal five cards to each player. This will be the player's hand. Then place the rest of the deck facedown between the pay-off piles. This is the stock.

Turn over the top card of each pay-off pile, and place it faceup on the pile. The player whose pile has the higher card on top goes first. If the cards have the same rank, shuffle each pay-off pile and try again.

The only cards visible to both players during the game will be the top cards of the pay-off piles. Whenever the top card is moved from the pay-off pile, turn the next one faceup to replace it.

Each player's goal is to move cards from his play-off pile onto one of the "center stacks" of cards. The center stacks do not exist at the beginning of the game but will be built during the game.

Players make the center stacks by moving cards from the pay-off pile, or from the player's hand, or from her "side-stack" (see below about building those) into a row that lines up with the stock.

The center stacks begin with an ace, followed by a 2-3-4, and so on, all the way up to queen. Suits don't matter when building center stacks. There may not be more than three center stacks on the table at a time.

Players also build side stacks during the game. These must line up with the pay-off piles. A player moves cards from his hand to a side stack when he cannot move any additional cards to a center stack.

On a player's turn, she must follow three steps:

♦ **FIRST:** If a player has played cards from her hand and has fewer than five cards left, she must draw as many cards from the stock as she needs to "refill" her hand back up to five cards.

♦ **SECOND:** Once she has five cards in her hand, she may play a card onto a center pile, either from her hand, from the top of her pay-off pile, or from the top of one of her side stacks. The player may play as many cards as she chooses, one at a time, onto the center stacks.

If she completes a center stack (that is, she fills it up all the way to a queen), her opponent must take that center stack and shuffle it into the stock. This will open up an empty space for a new center stack.

During his turn, if a player uses up all five cards in his hand without moving any to a side stack, he may refill his hand from the stock right away and continue playing.

♦ **THIRD:** When a player cannot move any more cards to a center stack, she may play a card from her hand onto one of her side stacks (or she may create a side stack, if she doesn't have one yet). A player may only have four side stacks at a time. When she moves a card from her hand onto a side stack, it should be placed faceup on the pile so that only the top card is visible.

It is possible to play cards off of a side stack, so it is a good idea to start four side stacks before placing cards on top of each other in a side stack. Remember, these piles form a row in line with the player's pay-off pile.

Any card from a player's hand may be moved onto a side stack. Cards from a pay-off pile or a center pile may never be moved to a side stack.

A player's turn ends when he plays a card onto a side stack.

The first player to move the last card in her pay-off pile onto a center stack wins.

If the stock pile runs out before this happens, the game is a draw—players gather up all the cards, shuffle, and play again.

CHAPTER 4

RUMMY GAMES

AUTHORS

TYPE OF GAME: RUMMY | **NUMBER OF PLAYERS:** 2 to 7

OBJECT: Capture the most cards to make the most "books"

Originally this game was played with special cards that had pictures of famous writers on them, which is why it's called Authors.

HOW TO PLAY

Deal out all the cards. It's okay if some players have a few cards more or less than others.

Players take turns asking for cards from other players. The goal is to collect "books" of cards. A book is all four cards of the same rank, such as four aces. If a player has books already in his hand after the deal, he can set those books faceup on the table in front of him.

This is a "book" of 5s.

When it's a player's turn, she can ask any other player for a specific card. The player who's asking must have at least one card of that rank in his hand. For example, she could ask another player if he has the 9 of hearts. She can only ask for this card if she's holding at least one card with the same rank in her hand—in this example, she must be holding at least one other 9. The player being asked must give over the card if she has it.

If a player asks for a card and receives it, she repeats her turn. It doesn't matter if she completes a book or not. As long as she is successful in asking for cards and receiving them, her turn continues.

When she asks a player for a card and that player doesn't have it, her turn ends, and the next player takes his turn.

The game continues this way, with players collecting and giving up cards. When a player completes a book (four cards of the same rank), he places the book faceup on the table in front of him.

The game ends when all the players have used up the cards in their hands. At that point, players count the number of books they've completed. The player with the most books wins the game.

DONKEY (PIG)

TYPE OF GAME: RUMMY **NUMBER OF PLAYERS:** 3 to 13

OBJECT: Capture four cards of the same rank, and avoid becoming the donkey (or the pig, depending on the title of the game that players choose to use)

There are several names for this game, but the idea is that it's named after an animal people like to make fun of.

HOW TO PLAY

Before starting, go through the deck and take out one set of four of a kind (such as four aces) for each player. These sets will form the deck for the game. Any set of four of a kind can be used for each player. For example, if there are four players, they could use a deck made up of four aces, four kings, four queens, and four jacks. Once the deck is made, set the rest of the cards aside—they won't be needed.

Deal four cards to each player. After looking at their hands, each player chooses one card from his hand, and passes it facedown to the player on his left. In other words, each player passes a card to the left and receives a card from the right.

Play continues like this until one player manages to collect four cards of the same rank. This player wins the round, but she shouldn't tell anyone yet.

Once a player's hand contains the four cards of the same rank, she has *almost* completed the round.

When she collects the fourth card to complete her hand, she should quietly place her cards facedown on the table and, without making a show of it, touch her finger to her nose and stay that way.

Any player who sees that she is touching her nose should also quietly place his cards on the table and touch his own nose. The last player left who isn't touching their nose is the donkey (or pig).

Some play that the donkey (or pig) now drops out of the game, and for the next round four cards of one rank are removed from the pack. Others play that players drop out when they have lost a certain number of times (six for donkey or three for pig). A losing player gets a letter with each loss until she spells "donkey" (or "pig").

MY SHIP SAILS AND MY BIRD SINGS

TYPE OF GAME: RUMMY | **NUMBER OF PLAYERS:** 4 to 7

OBJECT: Capture seven cards of the same suit

This simple card game is a lot of fun when played at high speed.

HOW TO PLAY

Deal seven cards to each player. After looking at their hands, each player chooses one card from his hand, and passes it facedown to the player on his left. In other words, each player passes a card to the left and receives a card from the right.

The goal is to collect seven cards of the same suit. The card that a player passes to his left should be in a suit that he isn't choosing to collect. For example, if a player sees that he has several hearts in his hand, and a few other cards in other suits, he should keep the hearts and place one of the other cards on the table.

Play continues like this until one player manages to collect seven cards of the same suit, for example, seven hearts or seven spades. When this happens, the player says, "My ship sails," shows his cards, and wins the game.

If there's a tie (if two players each manage to collect seven cards of the same suit at the same time), then whoever says, "My ship sails" first wins the game.

When a player obtains seven cards of the same suit, she should say, "My ship sails!"

VARIATION

There's a popular version of this game for up to twelve players that is known as "My Bird Sings."

Deal four cards to each player. The object in this version is to collect four cards of the same suit.

Play as in My Ship Sails, where each player passes a card to the left and receives a card from the right.

The first player to collect four cards of the same suit (such as four clubs or four diamonds), says, "My bird sings," shows her cards, and wins the game.

BASIC RUMMY

TYPE OF GAME: RUMMY   **NUMBER OF PLAYERS:** 2 to 6

OBJECT: Object: Make melds and score points

This is one of the most popular games in the history of card games, and there are many different versions of it. Its name even refers to an entire family of games. This is a simple, basic version.

Rummy became popular in the early 1900s and may have developed out of the older game Conquian or developed out of ancient Chinese games such as Mah-jongg.

HOW TO PLAY

For a two-person game, deal ten cards to each player. For three or four players, deal seven cards each, and for five or six players, deal six cards each. After dealing, place the deck facedown in the middle of the table, within everyone's reach. This is the stock.

Turn over the top card of the stock, and place it faceup next to the stock. This card starts the discard pile. Aces are high.

Players now take turns. On his turn, a player must take a card, either from the top of stock or the top of the discard pile. He can choose to "meld" or to "lay off" (see below) and then get rid of another card from his hand by placing it on the discard pile (known as "discarding").

If a player starts his turn by taking the top card from the discard pile, he may not discard that same card at the end of his turn. If he takes the top card from the stock, he may choose to discard it.

Melding and Laying Off

After picking up a card, if a player has a meld in his hand, he may lay these cards faceup on the table in front of him. This is known as "melding." Melds are either "sets" or "runs":

♦ **SET:** Three or more cards of the same rank is a set (also known as a "book"). For example, a "set of four" could be four sevens. A "set of three" could be three kings.

An example of a "meld." This type of meld is known as a "set."

♦ **RUN:** Three or more cards of the same suit, in order, is a run. For example, a "run of three" could be the 4-5-6 of diamonds. A "run of five" could be the 2-3-4-5-6 of spades.

The player doesn't have to meld if she doesn't want to. Sometimes, she might find it better to hold her cards so she can call "Rummy" (more on this below). If the player doesn't choose to meld cards during her turn, she may choose to lay off cards, which means she adds cards from her hand to a meld that's already faceup on the table.

Players can lay off cards onto any meld on the table, not just their own. For example, if there's a meld on the table that contains three 5s, the player may add another 5 to it. Or, if a meld contains the 7-8-9 of spades, he may add the 10 of spades or the 6 of spades to it.

Cards used in laying off can only come from a player's hand. A player cannot rearrange the melds on the table when laying off. For example, if one player has a meld of three 8s, and another has a 5-6-7 meld, the second player cannot take one of the 8s and move it over to her meld.

If a player finds that he can get rid of all of his cards in melds at once, along with one card for discarding, he may do so on his turn and call "Rummy." However, a player may only call "Rummy" before he has melded any cards. When a player calls "Rummy," he earns double the amount of points that he would normally earn for winning a hand.

If the stock runs out before anyone has run out of cards, the next player turns the discard pile facedown and then turns the top card over to start a new discard pile.

The first player to use up all of the cards she was dealt wins the round, which is known as "going out." The player must be able to discard in order to go out. In other words, if her last three cards are three aces, she can't place these faceup as a meld and win the hand. She must still have one card left over to discard.

In some versions of basic Rummy, a player doesn't have to discard to go out. A player's last card can go into a meld, or a lay off, or a discard, as long as the last card is played according to the regular rules.

As soon as a player goes out, the other players must count the number of cards they have left. Each of these cards counts for points, and all those points get added together for the winner's score. Remember, if the winner called "Rummy," her score is doubled. Points are counted in this manner:

♦ **ACE:** 1 point

♦ **NUMBER CARDS:** Points equal the value of their ranks. For example, 2s are worth 2 points, 3s are worth 3 points, and so on.

♦ **KING, QUEEN, OR JACK:** 10 points

After the score has been calculated and recorded, a new round begins.

Players should decide at the start of the first game whether they wish to play until someone collects a certain number of points, for example, 100 points, or to a certain number of rounds.

TONK

TYPE OF GAME: RUMMY	**NUMBER OF PLAYERS:** 2 to 6

OBJECT: Shed cards by forming "spreads" and collect all the counters

Another name for this popular game is Tunk, and it has similarities to some versions of Rummy.

HOW TO PLAY

If there are more than five players, use two decks shuffled together.

Every player starts with the same number of counters—any small items, such as coins or candies, will do. Any number of counters can be used. Players also need to agree on how many counters the winner of each round will receive from the other players. For example, players could agree that when someone wins a round, she wins two counters from each player.

Deal seven cards to each player. After dealing, place the deck facedown in the middle of the table, within everyone's reach. This is the stock.

Turn over the top card of the stock, and place it faceup on the table next to the stock. This card starts the discard pile.

Each player should now look at the cards in his hand and add up how many points he has. Points are counted in this manner:

♦ **ACE:** 1 point

♦ **NUMBER CARDS:** Points equal the value of their ranks. For example, 2s are worth 2 points, 3s are worth 3 points, and so on.

♦ **KING, QUEEN, OR JACK:** 11 points

If a player's cards add up to 49 or 50 points, he tells everyone else and lays his cards faceup so everyone can see. This ends the round right away and he "tonks"—that is, he wins twice as many counters as the winner would normally receive.

If more than one player has 49 or 50 points, it's a draw and no one wins any of the counters. The dealer gathers the cards and begins a new round.

If no one tonks, play begins. Players take turns, and a player has several choices on his turn:

♦ He may stop the round by laying all of his cards faceup on the table. This is called "dropping," and players usually do this when they think they have a *lower* number of points in their hand than any other player.

When this happens, everyone lays their cards faceup on the table and adds up their points. If the player who dropped does in fact have the lowest number of points, he wins the round and receives the regular number of counters that a player gets for winning the round.

If he doesn't have the lowest number

of points, he must pay twice the regular number of counters to the player who does have the lowest number of points. If there's a tie, he pays the same amount to each player with the lowest number.

The player with the lowest score wins the round and receives the regular number of counters from everyone else. If there's a tie, all the players with the lowest number win the round and receive counters.

♦ If a player doesn't drop, he must either draw a card from the stock (this is known as "plucking") or take the top card from the discard pile.

♦ After picking up a card, if a player has any "spreads" in his hand, he may lay these cards faceup on the table in front of him or she can add cards to spreads already on the table. Spreads are either "sets" or "runs":

♦ **SET:** Three or more cards of the same rank is a set (also known as a "book"). For example, a "set of four" could be four 7s. A "set of three" could be three kings.

♦ **RUN:** Three or more cards of the same suit, in order, is a run. For example, a "run of three" could be the 4-5-6 of diamonds. In this game, aces are low, and 2s are "wild," which means they can represent any card the player chooses.

Players can add cards onto any spread on the table, not just their own. For example, if there's a spread on the table that contains three 5s, the player may add another 5 to it. Or, if a spread contains the 7-8-9 of spades, he may add the 10 of spades or the 6 of spades to it. This is called "hitting." A player may only do this after he has drawn a card and before he discards.

The player ends his turn by placing a card from his hand faceup on the discard pile. There are five ways to end a round:

♦ A player tonks right after the deal.

♦ A player gets rid of his cards before discarding (either by laying down cards or adding to spreads). This is another way to tonk, and if a player does it, he wins the round and receives twice as many counters as a winner usually gets.

♦ A player runs out of cards when he discards during his turn. If this happens, he wins the hand and receives the number of counters everyone agreed upon at the start.

♦ A player drops his cards at the start of his turn.

♦ The stock runs out. When this happens, everyone lays their cards faceup on the table and add up their points. The player with the lowest number of points wins the hand and the regular amount of counters.

A player exits the game when he runs out of counters.

The player who wins all the counters wins the game.

WUSHYI FEN

TYPE OF GAME: RUMMY   **NUMBER OF PLAYERS:** 2 to 8

OBJECT: Be the first to collect five cards of the same suit and collect the most points

This Rummy-styled game comes from China, and another name for it is Fifty-One.

HOW TO PLAY

This game requires a deck with two jokers. The object is to collect five cards of the same suit. Jokers are "wild," that is, they can represent any card the player chooses.

Points are counted in this manner:

♦ **ACE:** 11 points

♦ **NUMBER CARDS:** Points equal the value of their ranks. For example, 2s are worth 2 points, 3s are worth 3 points, and so on.

♦ **KING, QUEEN, OR JACK:** 10 points

Before starting, players should decide on a total number of points to which they will play. For example, players could choose the number 500. In that case, the first player to earn 500 points would win the game.

Deal five cards to each player. After dealing, place the deck facedown in the middle of the table, within everyone's reach. This is the stock.

The first player takes the top card from the stock and adds it to the cards in her hand. Then she takes a card from her hand and places it faceup next to the stock. This card starts the discard pile.

Players now take turns. When it's a player's turn, he has two choices (when the discard pile has less than five cards) or three choices (when there are five cards in the discard pile):

♦ He can take the top card from the stock and add it to his hand. Then he must get rid of a card from his hand by placing a card faceup on the discard pile. As cards are added to the discard pile, the pile should be kept spread out so everyone can see all of the cards in it.

♦ He can take all of the cards in the discard pile. To do this, the player must first place the same number of cards from his hand faceup on the table as are in the discard pile. For example, if there are three cards in the discard pile, the player places three cards from his hand faceup on the table. Then he takes up the three cards in the discard pile. The three cards he placed on the table become the new discard pile.

There must never be more than five cards in the discard pile. As soon as there are five cards in it, each player has another choice during his turn:

♦ Take any card from the discard pile and add it to his hand. Then he must replace that card with another from his hand, by placing a card faceup on the discard pile.

As soon as there are five cards in the

discard pile, this decision becomes the first one that the players must make.

If a player doesn't choose to take a card from the pile, or to take the entire pile, but instead chooses to take the top card from the stock, then that player must also gather up the discard pile, turn those cards face down, and set them aside for the rest of the round. That player starts a new discard pile by getting rid of one card from her hand and placing it faceup next to the stock.

For example, there are five cards in the discard pile. The next person to have a turn after the discard pile receives its fifth card chooses to take a card from the discard pile and replace it with one from her hand. The player after that chooses to take up the entire discard pile and replace these cards with five cards from his hand. The next player chooses to take the top card from the stock. This player must then gather up the discard pile, turn the cards facedown, and set them aside. He then starts a new discard pile with a card from his hand, and the next player takes a turn.

When a player collects five cards of the same suit (such as five hearts), she has two choices:

♦ Take a card (either from the discard pile or the stock), and add a card to the discard pile. A player would do this if the five cards of the same suit are not worth many points. She would take a card in order to increase the point value of her hand.

When a player has five cards of the same suit, he can either "knock" or swap one of her five cards for the one on top of the discard pile.

♦ End the round by showing that she has five cards of the same suit. This is known as "knocking." When a player knocks, the round stops, and all the other players reveal their cards. Then everyone calculates their scores.

Having five cards of the same suit is called a "flush." If the player who knocked has the highest-scoring flush, then she wins double her amount of points.

If another player has a higher-scoring flush, then that player earns the point value of his hand plus the point value of the hand of the player who knocked, and the player who knocked loses the amount of points that her hand is worth.

The winner gathers up all of the cards, shuffles, and deals the next hand.

The player who reaches the total number of points decided on at the start of the game wins the entire game.

CONQUIAN

TYPE OF GAME: RUMMY   **NUMBER OF PLAYERS:** 2

OBJECT: Be the first to meld eleven cards

This is one of the oldest Rummy-style games. It may have started in the Southwestern United States, Mexico, or South America and has been played since at least the late 1800s.

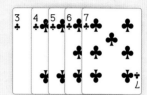

The two types of "melds."

HOW TO PLAY

Prepare the deck by removing all of the cards ranked 8, 9, and 10. Set those cards aside—they won't be used in this game. The deck should now contain forty cards. Aces are low.

The object is to create "melds." A meld is a set of three or more cards of the same rank, such as three 5s, or it can be a run of three or more cards of the same suit, in order, for example, the 3-4-5 of diamonds, or the 3-4-5-6-7 of clubs.

With this modified deck, jacks come after 7s, so a meld of 6-7-jack (all of the same suit) is allowed. However, melds cannot wrap around the end of the rank order, so a meld containing queen-king-ace would not be allowed. Kings are the highest-ranked cards, while aces are the lowest.

To win the game, a player must meld exactly eleven cards.

Deal ten cards to each player. After dealing, place the deck facedown in the middle of the table, within reach. This is the stock.

Each player can now look at her cards.

The player who didn't deal now turns over the top card of the stock. She doesn't add this card to her hand—instead, she must use this card to create a meld with cards from her hand, or she must use it to start the discard pile.

If she uses the card to create a meld, she places the melded cards faceup on the table in front of her. Then she must get rid of another card from her hand by placing it faceup on the table, which will be the start of the discard pile.

The player doesn't have to create melds even if she is able to. She may decide to wait (either because she wants to hold on to her cards and meld another time or to see what her opponent does first).

Next, the dealer takes his turn. He either uses the faceup card to create a meld, or he turns over the top card of the stock.

If he takes the faceup card for a meld, he must place the melded cards faceup on the table and then discard one card from his hand, by placing it faceup on the table. This card is now the start of the discard pile.

If he leaves the faceup card where it is, he takes the top card from the stock.

Now he has the same choice the first player did: either he uses this card to create a meld, or he places it faceup on the discard pile.

If he uses the card to make a meld, he places the meld faceup on the table, and then he places another card from his hand faceup on the discard pile.

Players continue taking turns in this way. In a player's turn she has two choices:

♦ Take the top card from the discard pile and use it for a meld. She places the melded cards faceup on the table and then places another card from her hand faceup on the discard pile.

Take the top card from the stock, and either use it for a meld or place it faceup on the discard pile. When a player has melds on the table, she may "borrow" cards from one meld to use in another, as long as the melds all remain intact.

For example, a player has a meld of 4-5-6-7 (all of the same suit), with another 7 among the cards in her hand, and she sees a 7 on the discard pile. She can take the 7 from the discard pile, and make a meld with the 7 in her hand and the 7 from the meld she has on the table. This gives her a meld of 7-7-7 and leaves the other meld intact as 4-5-6.

However, if a player has a meld on the table made up of jack-jack-jack, for example, and the opportunity comes up to create a meld of jack-queen-king by borrowing the jack from the other meld, he cannot do it because borrowing a jack would leave the meld as jack-jack, which is not a valid meld.

Remember, a meld must have at least three cards in it. A player may only borrow cards from her own melds and cannot touch her opponent's melds.

A player can also force her opponent to use a card (either the top card of the discard pile or the card turned over from the top of the stock) toward a meld he's already made, in order to block his plans and slow him down.

For example, if a player has a meld on the table containing 4-4-4, and there's a 4 on top of the discard pile, his opponent can force him (during his turn) to take the 4 from the discard pile and add it to his meld, making it 4-4-4-4.

A player cannot refuse this forced move. This counts as if he had chosen to pick up the 4, which means that he must now place another card from his hand faceup on the discard pile.

Play continues until a player manages to meld exactly eleven cards. Players were dealt only ten cards to start the game, so a player could be left with no cards left in her hand and all of her other cards melded.

In this case, she would then have to wait to find a card that will fit onto her existing melds, either as they are or by shifting them around (by borrowing cards from melds, as long as the melds remain intact).

This means, on her turn she would either use the top card from the discard pile for her eleventh card, or she would take the top card from the stock. If she can use it for her eleventh card, she wins. Otherwise, she places it faceup on the discard pile, and waits for her next turn.

If the stock runs out before anyone wins, the game is a tie.

LEVEL: HARD

CONTRACT RUMMY

TYPE OF GAME: RUMMY	NUMBER OF PLAYERS: 3 to 8

OBJECT: Be the first to meld all of your cards and have the lowest score

In Contract Rummy a single game takes place over the course of several deals, usually five to seven, and there is a different set of rules (known as the "contract") for each deal.

HOW TO PLAY

Players will need more than one deck of cards, depending on the number of players:

♦ For two to four players, use two decks

♦ For five or six players, use three decks

♦ For seven or eight players, use four decks

Each deck will also need two jokers. Shuffle all the decks together into one. Aces can be either low or high, depending on how the player chooses to use them. Jokers are "wild," which means they can represent any card the player chooses.

An entire game takes place over seven rounds—that is, cards will be dealt and played until someone wins the round, and this will happen seven times. The rules for winning each round are different and are known as "contracts."

The player's goal in each round is to collect the right combinations of cards to make "melds."

Melds are either "sets" or "runs":

♦ **SET:** Three or more cards of the same

rank is a set (also known as a "book"). For example, a "set of four" could be four 7s. A "set of three" could be three kings.

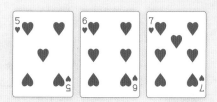

An example of a three-card set.

♦ **RUN:** Three or more cards of the same suit, in order, is a run. For example, a "run of three" could be the 5-6-7 of hearts. A "run of five" could be the 2-3-4-5-6 of spades.

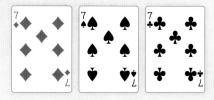

An example of a three-card run.

Each round has a "contract," which means that a player must make a specific collection of melds first, before she can make any other types of melds. For example, a round may have a contract of "a set of three, and a run of four," which means that the player would need to make both of those types of melds before she could make any other.

A card used in one set or run may not be used at the same time in another. For example, in a round where the contract is a set of three and a run of four, a player may use the 4 of spades, the 4 of diamonds, and the 4 of clubs to make the set, and the 4-5-6-7 of hearts to make the run. But if he is missing the 4 of diamonds, for example, he could not use the 4 of hearts in both the set of three and the run of four.

Only one wild card can be used in a single meld. For example, the meld 3-3-joker is allowed (where the joker represents a 3), but the meld 10-joker-joker is not allowed.

These are the contracts for each round:

♦ **FIRST ROUND:** Two separate sets of three; for example, 5-5-5 and ace-ace-ace

♦ **SECOND ROUND:** One set of three and one run of three; for example, 7-7-7 and 9-10-jack of hearts

♦ **THIRD ROUND:** Two separate runs of three; for example, 3-4-5 of spades and jack-queen-king of diamonds

♦ **FOURTH ROUND:** Three separate sets of three; for example, 5-5-5, 9-9-9, and king-king-king

♦ **FIFTH ROUND:** Two sets of three and one run of three; for example, ace-ace-ace, 4-4-4, and 7-8-9 of clubs

♦ **SIXTH ROUND:** One set of three and two runs of three; for example, 3-3-3, 7-8-9-10 of spades, and 5-6-7 of hearts

♦ **SEVENTH ROUND:** Three runs of four; for example, ace-2-3-4 of clubs, 7-8-9-10 of diamonds, and jack-queen-king-ace of spades

For the first four rounds, each player will be dealt ten cards facedown. For the last three deals, each player will be dealt twelve cards facedown. Each player can look at her own cards, but not anyone else's.

After dealing, place the rest of the deck facedown on the table. This is the stock.

The dealer takes the top card from the stock and places it faceup on the table. This card is called the "upcard," and it's the start of the discard pile.

Players take turns. On each turn, a player has two choices: either take the upcard or take the top card from the stock.

If a player doesn't take the upcard in her turn, she must wait until the other players have had a chance to "buy" it. Each player in turn is offered this chance.

If a player chooses to buy it, he takes the upcard, along with the top card from the stock pile. This extra card is the cost of buying the upcard.

After another player buys the upcard, or if all the other players refuse to buy it, the player whose turn it is continues by taking the top card from the stock.

Whichever card she picks up (upcard or top card from the stock), she may now choose to create melds. If she holds the cards needed to make a set or a run, she places those cards faceup on the table.

She may also choose to "lay off" cards, which means to add cards from her hand onto existing melds on the table. For example, if there's a run on the table made up of 3-4-5 of spades, a player may lay off the 6 of spades to that run.

If a meld contains a joker, a player can move it and change its rank in order to lay off cards.

For example, there's a meld made up of

the 4-5 of diamonds plus a joker (the joker represents the 6 of diamonds). A player holds the ace-2-6 of diamonds. During her turn, she can move the joker to the other end of the meld, making joker-4-5 of diamonds (so now the joker represents the 3 of diamonds). Now she can lay off the cards from her hand, creating the meld ace-2-joker-4-5-6 of diamonds.

A player doesn't have to create melds or lay off cards even if she has the cards to do so. She may choose to hold on to them.

A player must fulfill the contract for the round before she can create any other melds or lay off cards onto melds.

After melding or laying off, she must choose one card from her hand to discard. She places this card faceup on the discard pile (this card becomes the new upcard). If the player takes the upcard, she may not discard it on the same turn.

The first player to have no cards left in her hand after discarding wins the round. The round ends when there's a winner, and players calculate their points for the round.

The winner receives 0 points. The other players count up their cards to figure out their scores. Points are counted in this manner:

♦ **JOKER:** 15 points

♦ **ACE:** 15 points

♦ **NUMBER CARDS:** Points equal the value of their ranks. For example, 2s are worth 2 points, 3s are worth 3 points, and so on.

♦ **KING, QUEEN, OR JACK:** 10 points

After everyone writes down their score for the round, the dealer gathers up all the cards, and the next round begins. After all seven rounds, the player with the lowest number of points wins the game.

CHAPTER 5

TRICK-TAKING GAMES

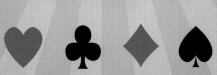

ROLLING STONE

TYPE OF GAME: TRICK-TAKING   **NUMBER OF PLAYERS:** 4 to 6

OBJECT: Shed all of your cards first and win tricks

This is an old game popular in England, France, and Germany. In France it's known as Enfle, and in Germany it's called Schwellen.

The fourth player will have to play a spade in order to "follow suit" for this trick.

HOW TO PLAY

If there are only four players, remove all of the cards ranked 2 through 6 from the deck and set them aside. This will leave a deck made up of thirty-two cards. If there are five players, remove the cards ranked 2 through 4. If there are six players, remove only the 2s. Aces are high.

Deal eight cards to each player, and set the rest of the deck aside.

This game is played in "tricks." A trick is another name for a round, when each player takes one turn. The first player in a round is said to be "leading the next trick."

The first player places a card from her hand faceup on the table. Each player takes a turn playing one card that matches the suit of the first card. This is called "following suit."

If a player cannot follow suit, she must take up all the cards that have been played in the trick and add them to her hand. Then she leads the next trick, which means she plays a card from her hand faceup on the table, and the other players each take a turn, following the suit of her card.

If every player manages to follow suit, then whoever played the highest-ranking card wins the round, which is also known as "winning the trick." The winner gathers up the cards that were played in the trick, and sets them aside. Then the winner leads the next trick.

The first player to shed all of the cards in his hand wins the game.

In some versions of this game, the winner of a round collects 1 point for each card left in the other players' hands. At the start of the game, players must decide how many points they will play to, and whoever reaches that target is the overall winner.

WHIST

TYPE OF GAME: TRICK-TAKING | **NUMBER OF PLAYERS:** 4 (in two teams of two)

OBJECT: Win seven or more tricks and be the first team to collect 5 points

This game dates back to the 1800s. It comes from Ruff and Honors, and later developed into Bridge.

HOW TO PLAY

Partners sit opposite each other at the table. Deal out all the cards among the players. Each player should have thirteen.

The final card, which belongs to the dealer, is turned faceup and placed on the table. The suit of this card is the "trump" suit. This card stays on the table until the dealer plays his first trick.

The first player starts a round (known as a "trick") by placing one card from his hand faceup on the table. Playing the first card in a trick is known as "leading the trick." Every player now takes a turn playing one card faceup on the table.

If a player has a card of the same suit as the card that led, she must play it. Otherwise, she may play any other suit.

After everyone has played one card, the person who played the highest-ranked card in the trump suit wins the trick. If no trump cards were played, the person who played the highest card in the suit that led wins the trick. Aces are high.

The winner of the trick gathers up the four cards played, turns them facedown, and sets them to one side. This player then leads the next trick.

Play continues until all of the cards have been used (there will be thirteen tricks played).

Teammates add together the number of tricks they won. The team who won the most tricks wins the round.

The winning team collects 1 point for every odd-number of tricks they won in excess of six tricks. In other words, if the winning team has seven tricks, they collect 1 point. If they have eight tricks, they still earn 1 point. If they have nine tricks, they earn 2 points. If they have eleven tricks, they earn 3 points, and so on.

The first team to collect 7 points wins the game.

VARIATIONS

Here are some popular variations on the basic game of Whist:

GERMAN WHIST

This version is for two players. The goal is to win the most tricks out of the last thirteen tricks played in the game.

Deal thirteen cards to each player. Set the remaining deck aside to become the stock pile. Turn the top card faceup, and place it on top of the facedown stock. The suit of this faceup card is the trump suit.

The player who didn't deal leads the first trick by playing any one of his cards faceup on the table. The other player must follow suit if possible.

If both cards are of the same suit, the higher card wins. If the two cards are of different suits, the first player wins the trick, unless the second player plays a trump. In that case, the trump wins.

The player who wins the trick takes the faceup card from the stock and adds it to his hand. The player who lost the trick then takes the facedown card directly below and adds it to his hand without showing it.

Turn over the next card in the stock, and place it faceup on the stock. The winner of the previous trick leads the next trick.

Play continues until the stock is used up. Players then play another thirteen tricks with the cards remaining in their hands.

Whoever wins the most tricks out of the final thirteen, wins the game.

German Whist has two components to its play. During the first half of play, the objective is to collect the best possible hand of cards for winning tricks. During the second half of play, the objective is to use that collection to win as many tricks as possible. In the first half of play, when cards are being won from the stock pile, the best strategy is to try to win or lose tricks based on whether the faceup card on the stock pile would benefit the player's hand. If it is a strong card, players should try to win the trick and collect the faceup card. If it is a weak card, players should try to lose the trick in order to collect the card below which may be better. During the second half of play, the strategy is to win as many tricks

as possible. This means collecting cards that are high-ranked in various suits and as many trump cards as possible during the first half of the play so a player's hand contains the best cards possible to take a maximum number of tricks during the last half of play.

KNOCKOUT WHIST

This version is suitable for at least three players, and as many as seven.

In Knockout Whist, each player receives seven cards to start. The dealer then turns over the top card of the deck, and the suit of this card is trump for the entire game.

The dealer leads the first trick, and each player must follow suit if they can. If they can't, they can either play a trump or play any other card from their hand. The winner of each trick leads the next.

When all the players have used up the cards they were dealt, the first round ends. Any player who didn't win a trick is knocked out of the game.

The player who won the most tricks in the first round becomes the dealer for the second round. In the second round, deal six cards to each player. After dealing, that player also has the right to choose the trump suit for that round.

At the end of each round, any player who didn't win a trick is knocked out. The player who wins the most tricks in a round becomes the dealer for the next round and, after dealing, chooses the trump suit for that round.

In each round, the number of cards dealt to each player is one less than the round before. The game ends when there is only one player left in the game (the game usually ends long before reaching the seventh round). That player is the winner.

ÉCARTÉ

TYPE OF GAME: TRICK-TAKING   **NUMBER OF PLAYERS:** 2

OBJECT: Be the first player to win 5 points

This trick-taking game (pronounced ay-car-tay) was popular in France in the late 1800s. It has similarities to Whist and Euchre.

HOW TO PLAY

Remove all of the cards ranked 2 through 6, creating a deck with thirty-two cards in it. For this game, the order of the cards, from lowest to highest, is 7-8-9-10-ace-jack-queen-king. The object of each round is to win at least three out of five possible tricks.

Deal five cards to both players, and set the remainder of the deck aside to become the stock. Turn the top card of the stock faceup. The suit of this card is the "trump" suit for the round. If this card is a king, the dealer automatically wins 1 point. During later rounds of play, if this point gives the dealer 5 points, he wins immediately and the game is over.

Before play begins, the player who didn't deal has the option of requesting an exchange of cards. This means getting rid of some or all of her cards and replacing them with fresh cards from the stock. A player makes this suggestion if she wants to improve her hand. It's usually best to keep high-ranking cards of the trump suit and to try to exchange low-ranking cards.

The dealer then has the option of

accepting or denying the request. If the dealer accepts, the nondealer passes any number of cards facedown to the dealer, who sets them aside and deals new cards from the stock to replace them. If an exchange is accepted, the dealer also must exchange at least one card from his hand.

The nondealer may keep making as many exchanges as she wishes, as long as the dealer continues to accept them. This exchange process ends and play starts when any of the following things happen:

♦ The nondealer chooses not to make an exchange and decides to lead the trick.

♦ The dealer refuses to make an exchange.

♦ There are no more cards remaining in the deck.

If the dealer doesn't want to accept her request, he is allowed to turn her down, and reject her request. If he does this, the dealer must win at least three tricks.

Before playing the first card in a trick, either player may win 1 point by showing that he has the king in the trump suit. It is not necessary to announce this if the player wishes to keep it a secret, but not declaring it sacrifices the point. If the card is not announced before playing the first card, the point cannot be earned later. The nondealer starts the round by playing one card from her hand. If the dealer can play a card of the same suit, he must do so. The higher card wins the trick.

If the dealer can't play a card of the same suit, he may still win the hand by playing a card in the trump suit (unless the first card played was a trump card, in which case, having no trump, he cannot win this trick).

If he doesn't have a card in the suit that was led, or the trump suit, he plays any other card from his hand.

If the dealer has a card that will win the trick, he must play it.

The winner of the trick collects both cards, places them in a stack in front of her on the table, and leads the next trick by playing any card from her hand that she wishes.

Play continues until the players have used all of their cards (that is, all five tricks have been played).

After, players calculate their scores:

♦ If a player wins three or four tricks, she earns 1 point.

♦ If a player wins all five tricks, it's called a "vole," and he earns 2 points.

♦ If either player chose to start the trick without exchanging any cards (either the nondealer didn't ask to make any exchanges or the dealer refused a request for an exchange), then that player had to win at least three tricks. If that player failed to win three tricks, the other player earns 2 points.

♦ If the dealer turned over a king at the start of the game, he won 1 point.

♦ If either player showed that they were holding the king in the trump suit at the start of the trick, he or she won 1 point.

The first player to earn 5 points wins the game.

If no one earns 5 points after the first five tricks, the deal switches to the other player, who gathers up all the cards and deals a new round.

EUCHRE

TYPE OF GAME: TRICK-TAKING

NUMBER OF PLAYERS: 4 (two teams of two, called partnerships)

OBJECT: Win at least three out of five tricks

Euchre (pronounced you-kur) is especially popular in Canada, the United States, England, and New Zealand. There are many variations. This is the most basic version.

HOW TO PLAY

This game is played with a partner. Make sure partners sit opposite one another at the table.

Before starting, remove all the cards ranked 2 through 8, and set them aside for the rest of the game. This creates a twenty-four-card deck.

Deal out five cards to each player. Then deal one card faceup on the table. This card's suit is the "trump" suit for the game.

This is the order of the cards in the deck, from highest to lowest:

♦ The jack of the trump suit, which is called the "Right Bower," is the highest card.

♦ The other jack in the same color as the trump suit, which is known as the "Left Bower," is the second highest.

♦ Then in order come the ace, king, queen, 10, and 9 in the trump suit.

♦ The other cards follow in regular order, from highest to lowest: ace, king, queen,

jack (the ones that aren't bowers), 10, and 9.

If hearts are the trump suit, the layout at the beginning of Euchre should look like this. The jack of hearts will be the highest card, and the jack of diamonds the second highest.

In clockwise order, each player takes a turn looking at his cards and announces if he accepts the faceup card's suit as the trump suit or if he passes.

If a player accepts the trump suit, he says, "I order it up." By accepting, a player is saying that he believes his team will win at least three tricks. This means that if a player holds several high-valued cards in the trump suit, it's usually a good idea to accept the trump.

If he doesn't want this suit as trump, he says, "pass."

If the first three players pass, the dealer can either accept the card as trump by saying, "I take it up," or pass by turning the card facedown.

If any player "orders up" the card, or if the dealer "takes it up," then the suit of the faceup card becomes the trump suit for the round. The dealer then adds this card to his hand and discards another card from his hand by placing it facedown on the table, and moving this pile to the side.

If all four players pass on the faceup card, the dealer turns the card over. In clockwise order, players have a chance to declare the trump suit of their choice, or pass.

If everyone passes for a second time, the dealer collects everyone's cards, and the deal passes to the player on the dealer's left, who shuffles and deals a new hand.

The team that accepts the trump suit is known as the "makers" for the game, and the other team becomes the "defenders." The makers must try to win three out of five tricks in the game.

After a trump suit has been selected for the game, but before anyone has had their first turn, any player can announce that he will play alone for the game.

A player will often do this if he has an unusually strong hand, and especially if he has a strong hand and his team is in danger of losing the game unless they are able to score points quickly.

If that happens, the player's partner sits out for this round. If the player going alone wins all five tricks, his team wins 4 points.

The player on the dealer's left leads. The player who leads the game can play any card faceup on the table. The card led doesn't have to be in the trump suit. After a card is led, the other players each take a turn in order.

Players must try to play a card faceup on the table of the same suit as the card that led. If a player doesn't have that suit in his hand, he may play any other card. The Left Bower (the jack that is the same color but different suit as the trump) is considered to belong to the trump suit, not its original suit.

After everyone has played one card, the player who laid the highest card wins. If any trumps were played, the winner is the player who laid the highest trump card. The player who wins the trick leads the next one.

When all five cards have been played, teams calculate how many points they've scored:

♦ If the makers win three or four tricks, they earn 1 point.

♦ If the makers win all five tricks, they earn 2 points.

♦ If the makers win less than three tricks, they have been "euchred," and the defenders earn 2 points.

♦ If one of the makers is playing alone and wins three or four, the makers earn 1 point.

♦ If one of the makers is playing alone and wins all five tricks, the makers earn 4 points.

♦ If one of the defenders is playing alone against a maker playing alone and wins at least three tricks, he has euchred the makers, and the defenders earn 4 points.

Euchre lasts several rounds, and the first team to collect 10 or more points wins the entire game.

HEARTS

TYPE OF GAME: TRICK-TAKING   **NUMBER OF PLAYERS:** 4

OBJECT: Avoid scoring points

This is a very popular game from the late 1800s, and it goes by many names, including Black Lady Hearts. The point is to avoid taking tricks, and especially tricks that contain penalty cards.

There are many versions of Hearts. This is a basic version. The rules are very simple, but the difficulty in Hearts is in the strategies.

HOW TO PLAY

Deal thirteen cards to each player. This will use up the entire deck. Aces are high. High-ranking cards are often called "strong" cards, and low-ranking cards are "weak."

After everyone receives their cards for the first round, each player must pass three of their cards facedown to the player on the left. Players can look through their cards to pick the ones they want to pass.

Here are some common strategies for passing cards:

♦ If a player holds mostly weak cards (that is, not a lot of high-valued cards that will win tricks and cost him points), he should pass off his strongest cards, especially kings, queens, and aces, so he won't get stuck with unwanted tricks.

♦ When passing off strong cards, it's also good to pass off a weak heart, in order to make it more difficult for another player to "shoot the moon" (more on this below).

♦ It's usually a good idea for a player to pass off high clubs and diamonds, and to try to get rid of all the cards he holds in those suits. That way, when one of those suits is led, a player can play any other card from his hand (that is, he doesn't have to wait for those suits to be led in order to play them from his hand).

♦ It's somewhat dangerous for a player to pass off hearts and spades, or try to get rid of all the cards he holds in those suits. Their spots in a player's hand may be filled by cards passed to him from another player, and these suits can create penalty points. They may also allow another player to "shoot the moon."

♦ If a player holds several hearts and spades, it's sometimes a good idea to hold on to them, in hopes of getting more and "shooting the moon."

♦ If a player holds a small number of spades, plus the queen of spades, he should pass off the queen. Otherwise, other players will play spades in order to flush out the queen, which will cause the player to take the trick and receive penalty points.

♦ When receiving cards, a player should try to guess what kind of hand the other player holds: for example, if she appears to be trying to get rid of all the cards in a particular suit, or if she seems to be keeping certain suits (that is, if she hasn't passed along any cards in a particular suit).

After the first round, the deal passes to the player on the dealer's left. Then, after the second round's cards are dealt out, everyone passes three cards again, but this time it's to the player on the right. After the third round's cards, pass cards to the players sitting opposite one another. After the fourth round, no one passes cards. If the game continues past four hands, the cycle begins again with the next deal, and everyone passes cards to the player on the left.

When players receive their cards, they look through them for the 2 of clubs. Whoever has that card goes first by placing it faceup on the table. Play moves to the left around the table.

The next three players now take a turn playing one card faceup on the table. Players must follow suit if they are able (that is, play a card of the same suit as was led). In the first trick, out of the four cards faceup on the table, the highest-ranked club wins the trick.

The player that wins the first trick collects the four cards and places them in a pile facedown next to her. She then leads the next trick by placing a card from her hand faceup on the table. If a player doesn't have any cards in the right suit, he can play any other card. After everyone has played a card, the highest card in the suit that led wins the trick and leads the next one.

Players aren't allowed to lead with a heart, until someone else has already played one (which is only done if another player doesn't have a card in the leading suit), or if a player's hand contains nothing but hearts.

During the scoring phase of the game, players collect penalty points for any hearts they win. Therefore, hearts are often known as "penalty cards."

The other penalty card in this game is the queen of spades (see scoring below).

Because the queen of spades is a penalty card, players will often try to lead a trick with a lower-valued spade, in order to get someone to play the queen sooner. This tactic is known as "smoking out the queen" or "fishing for the queen."

At the end of each round, someone should record the score of each player on a piece of paper:

♦ A player collects 1 point for every heart they win in a trick.

♦ The player who wins the queen of spades in a trick collects thirteen points.

♦ If a player wins all of the penalty cards (that is, all of the hearts and the queen of spades), this is "shooting the moon," and he either reduces his score by 26 points, or he can choose to increase everyone else's score by 26 points.

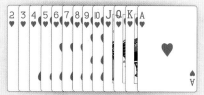

Winning all of these cards (the penalty cards) is "shooting the moon."

The game continues until one player collects 100 or more points. When that happens, the player with the lowest overall score wins the game.

Here are some more useful strategies:

♦ Players should try to remember what cards have already been played, and what they have passed. This will help them estimate whether or not they are likely to receive cards that will help or hurt their hand. For example, if they have seen the queen of spades, or several hearts and spades already, they are less likely to receive them.

♦ A good way to avoid taking tricks is known as "ducking." To do this, a player lays down his highest card after a higher card was played by someone else.

For example, if a trick contains the 8, 9, and jack of clubs, a player could play the 10 of clubs. If a player holds the ace, he can't get rid of it by ducking. Eventually, when someone else leads clubs, the player will have to play the ace and risk collecting any penalty cards played in that trick.

♦ A good way to avoid getting the queen of spades is to hold it. If a player holds several spades plus the queen, he can avoid other players fishing for the queen because he has several other spades with which to follow suit when necessary.

If he has already gotten rid of one or more of the other suits in his hand, once all the other players run out of spades, the player holding the queen can play it safely.

Also, if he sees the ace or king of spades played in a trick, that's a good time to play the queen, since either higher card will beat the queen.

♦ If a player holds the queen and a small number of other spades, it's sometimes a good idea to try to win a trick in another suit (that is, any suit other than spades). That way, he will be able to lead the next suit.

He should then continue leading non-spades until he has cleared his hand of them. Then, when another player leads with a suit he doesn't hold, the player holding the queen of spades can play it safely. Whoever wins the trick will take the queen.

♦ If a player doesn't have the queen of spades, he should try to get rid of the ace and king of spades because they win the queen easily.

♦ If a player holds high cards, he should risk taking tricks with them early in the hand, in order to get rid of them. There's usually less chance of someone playing the queen early in the game.

♦ A good hand is usually one that contains a lot of low-ranked cards and no queen of spades. A player with a hand like this will be able to duck most of his cards.

The risk is that if he holds many low cards and no queen of spades, another player may hold a lot of high-valued cards plus the queen, which would encourage that player to shoot the moon.

♦ If a player is stuck holding several high-valued cards (such as high hearts, or the queen of spades), it's sometimes a good strategy to keep some low cards in those same suits (that is, if he holds high hearts, he should try to keep some low ones, or if he holds the queen of spades, he should try to hold some low spades).

That way, when other players lead those suits, he can avoid playing the high cards and winning the tricks. He can wait and try to dump them when a suit that he doesn't have is led.

OBJECT: Be the first team to reach 21 points

This is part of a family of games known as All Fours and High-Low Jack. Other names for this variation include Setback and Auction Pitch. There are several versions of this game, and this is the most basic one.

HOW TO PLAY

Partners sit opposite one another.

Deal six cards to each player. After the deal, players participate in one round of bidding, where each team declares how many of the following four prizes they promise to win:

♦ **THE "HIGH" PRIZE:** This goes to the team who wins the trick that contains the highest-ranked card in the trump suit.

♦ **THE "LOW" PRIZE:** This goes to the team who wins the trick that contains the lowest-ranked card in the trump suit.

♦ **THE "JACK" PRIZE:** This goes to the team who wins the trick containing the jack of the trump suit.

♦ **THE "GAME" PRIZE:** This goes to the team who collects the most card points in tricks at the end of the game (see below for more about winning tricks). If there's a tie, no one wins the Game prize.

The card point values are as follows:

♦ **ACE:** 4 points

♦ **KING:** 3 points

♦ **QUEEN:** 2 points

♦ **JACK:** 1 point

♦ **TEN:** 10 points

When making their bids, players choose one of the following:

♦ **BID OF TWO:** This means the team promises to win two of the prizes.

♦ **BID OF THREE:** This means the team promises to win three of the prizes.

♦ **BID OF FOUR:** This means the team promises to win all four prizes.

♦ **SMUDGE BID:** This means the team promises to win all four prizes, as well as all six tricks in the round.

♦ **PASS:** Players may also choose to pass, which means that they don't make a bid.

Each player except the dealer must make a higher bid than the previous bid or pass.

The dealer makes the last bid and is allowed to bid the same amount as the highest bid. This is "stealing the bid."

If the first three players all pass, the dealer must make a bid of at least two. This is known as a "force bid."

The player who bids the highest is the "pitcher" for the round, and the pitcher's team becomes the "declaring team."

The declarer's bid becomes the main bid for the round. This is the only bid that matters when it comes to scoring points at the end of the round.

The pitcher chooses the trump suit and plays the first card by laying one card in the trump suit faceup on the table.

The next three players must now play one card faceup on the table. If they have a card in the trump suit, they must play it. When all four cards are on the table, the highest card wins the "trick."

The player who wins the trick gathers up all four cards and keeps them in a stack facedown next to him. The winner of the first trick leads the next trick, which means he must place one card faceup on the table.

After the first trick, the winner can lead a card in any suit. The next three players must now play one card faceup on the table, of the same suit as the card that led the trick. If a player doesn't have a card in that suit, he can play any other suit.

After all four players have taken a turn, the highest card in the suit that led the trick wins, unless cards in the trump suit were played. In that case, the highest card in the trump suit wins the trick.

Keep playing until everyone has used up the cards in their hand—six tricks in all. After that, calculate who wins the High, Low, Jack, and Game prizes. Each of those prizes is worth 1 point.

If the declaring team fulfills their bid, they collect points for all the prizes they win. These are different from the card points used to calculate who wins the Game prize. For example, if the declaring team bid two, and end up winning four prizes, that team collects 4 points. If a team successfully completes a smudge, they win 5 points.

If the team manages to win all four prizes, as well as all six tricks, but didn't bid smudge, they only collect 4 points.

If the declaring team doesn't manage to make their bid, they lose the value of the bid. For example, if a team bid three but only won two prizes, the team loses 3 points.

If a team bids smudge and doesn't make it, they lose 5 points.

Regardless of whether the declaring team makes its bid or not, the non-declaring team also collects 1 point for any prize they win.

After writing down the score for each team, gather up the cards, give them to the new dealer, and play another round. Keep adding points to (or subtracting points from) the team scores after each round.

A team wins the game if they collect 21 or more points at the end of a round when they are the declaring team.

If a team collects 21 points or more in a round when they are not the declaring team, or when they make a bid but don't fulfill it, play continues either until the team finishes in which they fulfill their bid or until the other team wins.

This means it's possible for a team to win even though it has fewer points at the end of the game than the other team. For example, if one team finishes a round with a total of 23 points, but they didn't make their bid, while the other team finishes with 19 points, in the next round, the second team could finish with 21 points and make their bid, while the first team finishes with 26 points.

The team who has 21 points wins the game because they collected the required number of points and made their bid in the same round.

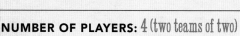

SPADES

TYPE OF GAME: TRICK-TAKING **NUMBER OF PLAYERS:** 4 (two teams of two)

OBJECT: Be the first team to reach 500 points

Spades is similar to Whist and Hearts. It is part of a family of games known as Bad Whist. There are many variations of Spades. This is the basic version.

HOW TO PLAY

Teammates sit opposite one another at the table. Deal out all the cards among the players. Each player will receive thirteen.

Players should look at their cards and say how many rounds (or "tricks") he promises to win. This is a bid. A bid can be any number from 0 to 13.

The player on the dealer's left makes the first bid. After all four players make their bids, partners add their bids together to come up with the bid for their team.

Make sure to write down each team's bid, so it will be easier to remember.

Usually, players make bids based on how may high-ranked cards they are holding (that is, cards that are likely to win tricks).

Aces are high. Spades are always the trump suit. This means any spade will be the highest card played in a hand. If more than one spade is played, then the highest-ranking of the spades wins.

If a player makes a bid of zero, this is called "Nil." This means she will try to lose every hand played in the game, and she does not want to win any tricks.

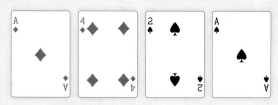

If more than one spade is played, then the highest ranking spade wins. Here, it is the ace of spades.

If she succeeds at this, she earns a bonus, but if she fails, there's a penalty. When a player bids nil, the bonus or penalty depends only on how many tricks she wins or loses as an individual, and doesn't include her partner's performance.

When bidding nil, it is important for a player to either have a very weak hand or to trust that his partner has a strong enough hand to stop him from collecting tricks.

The player on the dealer's left makes the first play (known as "leading the trick"), by laying any card he wishes (except for a spade) faceup on the table.

The other players must then each place one card faceup on the table in turn. Players must try to play a card that has the same suit as the first card played. If they are unable to do so, they may play a card in any other suit.

After everyone has played one card, the player who laid the highest card wins the trick. If more than one trump card is played, the one with the highest rank wins. If no one plays a trump card, the highest-ranked card in the suit that led wins.

The winner of the hand gathers up the cards played and sets them to one side and then leads the next trick.

A player may not lead with a spade until another player has played a spade in a hand, or unless he has no other cards but spades in his hand.

Continue playing until all of the cards in the deck have been used, and then add up the number of tricks each team won.

If a team took at least as many tricks as they bid, they win the number of points equal to 10 times their bid. For example, if their bid was 5, they would win 50 points.

Any tricks that a team wins above their bid (these are called "overtricks") count for 1 point each.

However, for every ten overtricks that a team wins, the team must subtract 100 points from their score. It's useful to keep track of how many overtricks each team collects as the game progresses so they will know when they hit ten.

If the team doesn't make its bid (that is, if they don't collect as many tricks as they promised), they lose 10 points for every trick they bid (so an unmet bid of 5 would be worth –50 points).

If a player successfully bids nil, he collects 50 points, as well as the points won or lost by his partner.

If he's unsuccessful at his bid of nil (that is, if he bid nil and then won a trick), he loses 100 points, but his team can still collect points for tricks won by his partner.

If a player bids nil and wins tricks, these don't count toward his partner's bid.

This game is played over several rounds and continues until one team collects 500 points to win the game.

INDEX